SPECTRUM®

Word Problems
Grade 5

Published by Spectrum®
an imprint of Carson-Dellosa Publishing LLC
Greensboro, NC

Spectrum®
An imprint of Carson-Dellosa Publishing LLC
P.O. Box 35665
Greensboro, NC 27425 USA

ISBN 978-1-6244-2731-2

04-306157811

Table of Contents Grade 5

Table of Contents, continued

Check What You Know

Adding and Subtracting through 6 Digits

Read the problem carefully and solve. Show your work under each question.

A TV station surveyed its viewers to find their favorite sport. The survey showed that 157,238 people chose basketball, 95,215 people chose football, 63,482 people chose baseball, 8,967 people chose soccer, 4,251 people chose tennis, 294 people chose polo, and 53 people chose rugby.

1. How many people surveyed chose either polo or rugby as their favorite sport?

   _____ people

2. What is the difference between the number of people who chose basketball and the number of people who chose football?

   _____ people

3. What is an estimate of the number of people who like soccer or tennis best? Round the numbers to the nearest thousand.

   about _____ people

4. Sharla notices the three sports that are chosen the most. How many people in total chose basketball, football, or baseball?

   _____ people

5. May looks for the three sports that are chosen least. How many people in all chose tennis, polo, or rugby?

   _____ people

6. Roberto calculates the difference between the number of people who chose football and the number of people who chose soccer. What is the difference?

   _____ people

NAME _____

Lesson 1.1 Adding and Subtracting 2 and 3 Digits

Read the problem carefully and solve. Show your work under each question.

Carla's Fabric Shop has many different patterns of fabric for sale. The shop sells 227 patterns made of cotton, 24 patterns made of rayon, 18 patterns made of wool, and 35 patterns made of silk.

> **Helpful Hint**
>
> Read each question carefully before you decide which numbers to add or subtract. Check each answer to be sure it makes sense.

1. Julia wants to buy patterns made of cotton or wool. How many total patterns are made of cotton or wool at the fabric shop?

   _____ patterns

2. Sandra does not like the feel of cotton fabrics. She likes fabrics made of rayon or silk. How many total patterns made of rayon or silk are at the fabric shop?

   _____ patterns

3. Kim wants to know how many patterns are not made of rayon or wool. How many patterns in the store are not made of rayon or wool?

   _____ patterns

4. Wilma sees that two fabrics in the shop have the fewest choices of patterns. How many patterns in total are made of these two fabrics?

   _____ patterns

5. Marta compares the number of patterns made from cotton with the number of patterns made from wool. How many more patterns are made from cotton than from wool?

   _____ patterns

Lesson 1.2 Adding and Subtracting 3 through 6 Digits

Read the problem carefully and solve. Show your work under each question.

Three towns are located near the city of Easton. The towns are Bransom, Newville, and Sterling. The city of Easton has a population of 576,283. Bransom has a population of 4,211, Newville has a population of 919, and Sterling has a population of 652.

Helpful Hint

When you subtract large numbers, first subtract the ones, then the tens, the hundreds, the thousands, and so on.

1. Sheryl lives in Easton. She thinks she would like to live in one of the small towns. How many more people live in Newville than in Sterling?

_____ people

2. Mr. Ruiz teaches fifth grade math. One student guesses that 6,000 people altogether live in Bransom and Newville. How many people actually live in the two towns?

_____ people

3. Tomas is comparing the populations of the largest city and the smallest town. How many more people live in Easton than in Sterling?

_____ people

4. A water company needs to provide water for all the people in Easton and Bransom. How many people live in the two towns?

_____ people

5. The doctors of Newville and Sterling want to build a new emergency room to serve the people in the two towns. How many people would the emergency room serve in all?

_____ people

Lesson 1.3 Adding 3 or More Numbers (3 to 6 Digits)

Read the problem carefully and solve. Show your work under each question.

Gnus (*nus*) are wild animals that look like a mix of a cow and a horse. Gnus live in African grasslands. Gamekeepers are counting the herds of gnus in one area. Herd A has 383,610 gnus. Herd B has 107,941 gnus. Herd C has 58,735 gnus. Herd D has 5,479 gnus. Herd E has 224,878 gnus.

Helpful Hint

When you add large numbers, first add the ones, and then the tens. Then, add the hundreds. Then, add the thousands. Keep going until all the numbers are added.

1. Mr. Lee asks Tran how many gnus are in the three smallest herds. What is the total number of gnus in the three smallest herds?

   _____ gnus

2. Linda says that there are about 700,000 gnus in the three largest herds. How many gnus altogether were actually counted in the three largest herds?

   _____ gnus

3. Miriam adds together all the herds with less than 300,000 gnus. What is the total number of gnus in these herds?

   _____ gnus

4. Jorge finds the sum of four of the herds of gnus, not counting Herd C. What is that sum?

   _____ gnus

5. Gamekeepers are writing a report about the gnus in their area. How many gnus did they count in total?

   _____ gnus

Lesson 1.4 Estimating Sums and Differences

Read the problem carefully and solve. Show your work under each question.

Acme Pencil Company ships boxes of pencils to different companies. This week, Acme ships 1,534 boxes to Sizemore Sales. Then, Acme ships 3,795 boxes to Morgan Company. It sends 12,478 boxes to Big Mart Retailers. Also, Acme sends 38,722 boxes to Every State Sellers.

Helpful Hint

Before you estimate a sum or difference, round each number to the greatest place value the numbers have in common.

1. Sergio is a sales manager for Acme. He compares the largest and smallest shipments of boxes this week. What is an estimate of the difference?

   about _____ boxes

2. Carmen estimates the total number of pencil boxes in the two largest shipments this week. About how many boxes were in these two shipments?

   about _____ boxes

3. Gary compares the two smallest shipments. About how many more boxes of pencils were shipped to Morgan Company than to Sizemore Sales?

   about _____ boxes

4. About how many more boxes of pencils were shipped to Big Mart Retailers than to Morgan Company this week?

   about _____ boxes

Check What You Learned

Adding and Subtracting through 6 Digits

Read the problem carefully and solve. Show your work under each question.

In the city of Agate, the voters are members of several political parties. 134,977 voters are Loyalists, 86,356 are Titans, 4,318 are Patriots, 988 are Rankers, and 93 are Junkers.

1. Raymond compares the political parties with the greatest and the least number of voters. What is the difference in the number of voters in these two parties?

_____ voters

2. The Loyalists have more voters than all of the other parties combined. What is the total number of voters in all the other parties?

_____ voters

3. Tracy thinks that there are less than 5,000 total voters in the three smallest parties. How many voters altogether are in the three parties?

_____ voters

4. Juan hears that 12,000 voters are going to leave the Loyalist party. How many members will the Loyalist party have if 12,000 members leave?

_____ members

5. Margot is asked to guess the total number of voters in the two largest parties. What is a good estimate?

about _____ voters

6. All the members of the Patriots party decide to join the Loyalists. How many voters are in the Loyalists and Patriots combined?

_____ voters

Check What You Know

Multiplying through 4 Digits by 3 Digits

Read the problem carefully and solve. Show your work under each question.

Students in Thornton's schools are collecting soda cans and bottles for a charity drive. They have a contest to see which students and which schools collect the most cans and bottles.

1. Elmhurst has 328 students. Each student collects 28 cans during the contest. How many cans do the students collect?

_____ cans

2. At Oakwood, 7 students collect 125 bottles each. How many bottles do these students collect in all?

_____ bottles

3. Park Central has 156 students. Each student collects 114 bottles. How many bottles do they collect in total?

_____ bottles

4. The contest lasts 15 weeks. One student, Raul, collects 33 cans per week. How many cans does Raul collect during the contest?

_____ cans

5. During the contest, 2,254 students each collect 24 bottles. How many bottles do they collect in all?

_____ bottles

6. When the contest ends, 11 schools have collected an average of 8,995 cans per school. What is an estimate of the total number of cans collected by the schools?

about _____ cans

Lesson 2.1 Multiplying 1, 2, and 3 Digits by 1 Digit

Read the problem carefully and solve. Show your work under each question.

A computer game company held a contest on Saturday. The company kept track of how many hours each person participated in the contest. 27 people played for 2 hours. 113 people played for 3 hours. 73 people played for 4 hours. 35 people played for 5 hours. 18 people played for 6 hours.

Helpful Hint

To find the total time a group of people spends on an activity, multiply the number of people by the time each one spends on the activity.

1. Which group of players had the most number of hours? How many total hours did they play?

   the group of _____ people

   _____ hours

2. Some of the participants played in the contest for 4 hours. How many total hours did these participants play?

   _____ hours

3. The largest group had more than 100 players. How many total hours did these players participate in the contest?

   _____ hours

4. One group of participants played for the shortest amount of time. How many total hours did this group play?

   _____ hours

5. How many total hours did the group with 35 participants play in the contest?

   _____ hours

Lesson 2.2 Multiplying 2 and 3 Digits by 2 Digits

Read the problem carefully and solve. Show your work under each question.

At Sparrow Hospital, the nurses work 12-hour shifts, three days per week. There are 4 weeks in an average month and 12 months in a year. At the hospital, 23 nurses work during each shift.

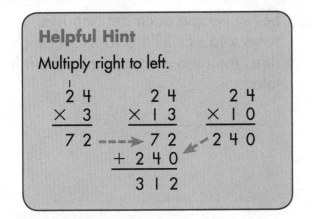

Helpful Hint

Multiply right to left.

1. During one shift, 23 nurses work 12 hours each. How many total hours do the nurses work on the shift?

   _____ hours

2. In an average month, each nurse works a total of 12 days. How many total hours does each nurse work in an average month?

   _____ hours

3. Lucia is a nurse at the hospital. With overtime, she works an average of 150 hours each month. How many hours does Lucia work in a year?

   _____ hours

4. Nurse Tanya works an extra day each month. How many days does Tanya work each year?

   _____ days

Lesson 2.3 Multiplying 4 Digits by 1 and 2 Digits

Read the problem carefully and solve. Show your work under each question.

Giant Auto Sales Lot has a bonus plan for the salespeople. For $50,000 in total sales, a salesperson gets a bonus of $2,250. For $75,000 in sales, the bonus is $3,475. The bonus for $100,000 is $4,775.

Helpful Hint

When you multiply a number with a 5 in the ones place, the product always has a 0 or a 5 in the ones place.

1. Eleven salespeople each sell $50,000 worth of cars this month. How much bonus money in total does Giant Auto pay them?

   _____

2. This month, four salespeople each have sales worth $100,000. What total amount of money in bonuses does the company pay them?

   _____

3. Seven people each get bonuses for sales totals of $75,000. How much does the auto company pay them in total?

   _____

4. The company sets a goal for 15 people to have sales worth $50,000 next month. How much money does the company plan to pay them in bonuses?

   _____

5. Last month, three people each had sales of $75,000. What is the total of bonuses that Giant Auto paid?

   _____

Lesson 2.4 Multiplying 3 and 4 Digits by 3 Digits

Read the problem carefully and solve. Show your work under each question.

A computer plant keeps track of how many parts its workers make per week. An average worker makes 160 parts per week. A quick worker makes 212 parts per week. A month has 4 weeks. The workday is split into three shifts of 8 hours each.

Helpful Hint

To find the answer to a word problem, first restate the problem in your own words. Then, look for the information that is needed to answer your question.

1. At the plant, 1,374 workers are in the average group. How many parts do they make in a week?

   _____ parts

2. There are 237 workers in the quickest group at the plant. How many parts do they make in a week?

   _____ parts

3. On a shift, there are 458 average workers. Each worker makes 640 parts in a month. How many parts altogether do these workers make in a month?

   _____ parts

4. In the quickest group there are 237 workers. They each make 848 parts per month. How many parts altogether do these workers make in a month?

   _____ parts

5. After additional training, each average worker now makes 172 parts per week. Now, how many parts in all do the 1,374 average workers make per week?

   _____ parts

Lesson 2.5 Estimating Products

Read the problem carefully and solve. Show your work under each question.

A hardware store sells many kinds of products. The owners of the store often estimate how fast the products are selling, so they know when to buy more of each product they sell.

Helpful Hint

To estimate the product of two numbers, round each number to its highest place value.

Suppose you want to estimate the product of 837 times 36. Round 837 to 800. Round 36 to 40. Then, multiply 800 times 40. The product is 32,000.

1. The store sells an average of 17 boxes of nails per day. The store is open 311 days per year. About how many boxes of nails are sold in a year?

   about _____ boxes

2. Simon sells about 2 tape measures per week. There are 104 weeks in 2 years. About how many tape measures does Simon sell in 2 years?

   about _____ tape measures

3. Jason sells an average of 56 faucets per month. About how many faucets does he sell in 48 months?

   about _____ faucets

4. Pearl sells an average of 14 brooms per month. What is an estimate for the number of brooms she sells in a year?

   about _____ brooms

Check What You Learned

Multiplying through 4 Digits by 3 Digits

Read the problem carefully and solve. Show your work under each question.

The city of Alford has 315 firefighters. During each shift, firefighters are at the station for 3 days in a row. Then, they have 4 days off. They also get 4 weeks of vacation per year.

1. Each firefighter works 144 days per year. How many total days do all of the firefighters work?

_____ days

2. All the firefighters get paid for vacation each year. How many total weeks of vacation does the city pay for firefighters each year?

_____ weeks

3. Firefighters have 221 days off per year. A day has 24 hours. How many total hours off does each firefighter have per year?

_____ hours

4. Julia knows that a firefighter works 72 hours every week and 48 weeks per year. About how many total hours does each firefighter work per year?

about _____ hours

5. There are 72 hours in 3 days. How many total hours do 125 firefighters work in 3 days?

_____ hours

6. Each firefighter in Alford misses 3 days of work per year because of sickness. How many days in total do all of the firefighters miss per year?

_____ days

Check What You Know

Dividing through 5 Digits by 2 Digits

Read the problem carefully and solve. Show your work under each question.

A big coin show is held at a local meeting hall. Coin collectors buy and sell coins at the show. Thousands of coins are available. The price for a coin ranges from a few cents to thousands of dollars.

1. Mr. Ahmed takes 6 students to the show. In total the students buy 48 coins. How many coins does each student buy, if they each buy the same number of coins?

   _____ coins

2. Delia has 39 pennies. She divides the pennies evenly into 4 stacks. How many coins are left over?

   _____ pennies

3. One collector sells 144 coins to 16 people. If each person buys the same number of coins, how many coins do they each buy?

   _____ coins

4. Thirty coin collectors bring 627 coins to the show. If you divide 627 by 30, what is the exact quotient?

   _____

5. There are 92 coin dealers at the show. The coin dealers spend a total of $38,750. How much does each dealer spend on average, rounded to the nearest dollar?

   about _____

Lesson 3.1 Dividing 2, 3, and 4 Digits by 1 Digit

Read the problem carefully and solve. Show your work under each question.

Middle City Hardware is having a big sale. The staff workers are putting tools and other items in groups for the sale.

Helpful Hint

Some division problems have a **remainder**. The remainder is any the number that is left when a divisor does not divide a dividend exactly. The remainder is always less than the divisor.

1. The store is selling 3 gallons of paint for the price of one. If the store has 122 gallons to sell, how many gallons will not be in a group of 3?

_____ gallons

2. Josie's boss gives her 258 bolts. Her boss says to put the bolts in bags of 9 bolts each. How many full bags of bolts will she have?

_____ bags

3. Chad has 137 screwdrivers. Chad puts them in sets of 4. How many screwdrivers will be left over when he is finished?

_____ left over

4. Special sale items are worth $7,527 in all. The sale will last for 3 days. How much money will the store make per day if the sales are equal each day?

_____

Lesson 3.2 Estimating Quotients

Read the problem carefully and solve. Show your work under each question.

The Quick Haul Trucking Company makes local deliveries. The shipping manager divides all of the boxes into various shipments. Sometimes, the manager makes estimates for the shipments.

Helpful Hint

To estimate a quotient, round the dividend into a number that is easily divided by the divisor.

To estimate the quotient of 45 divided by 7, first round 45 into 42. Then, a good estimate of the quotient is 6.

1. Quick Haul delivers 133 boxes to 3 stores. Each store gets about the same number of boxes. Estimate the number of boxes going to each store.

about _____ boxes

2. Quick Haul trucks can carry 22 boxes of one size. There is a shipment of 83 boxes to deliver. Estimate the number of truckloads for the shipment.

about _____ truckloads

3. Quick Haul delivers 103 lamps to 7 stores. If each store gets about the same number of lamps, about how many lamps will each store get?

about _____ lamps

4. A basket company ships 1,623 baskets to 9 sellers. Each seller receives about the same number of baskets. To the nearest ten, about how many baskets does each seller receive?

about _____ baskets

5. Quick Haul was paid $875 for 4 equal shipments. To the nearest $10, about how much did Quick Haul get paid for each shipment?

about _____

Lesson 3.3 Dividing 2 Digits by 2 Digits

Read the problem carefully and solve. Show your work under each question.

The manager at the plant sets the work schedule. To do this, the manager divides the year into different periods of time. The factory has two 8-hour shifts, 5 days a week. There are 56 workers per shift. The plant has 23 workstations.

Helpful Hint

To divide a number by a 2-digit number, first use mental math. In the problem $24\overline{)78}$, a good guess is the quotient is less than 4. (24 rounds to 20 and $4 \times 20 = 80$.) Try multiplying 24×3. The product is 72. Next, subtract 72 from 78 to find the remainder.

1. There are 52 weeks in a year. The plant runs for 12 months. How many weeks are left when 52 weeks are divided by 12 months?

   _____ weeks

2. The plant runs 80 hours a week. A day has 24 hours. How many days does the plant run each week? (Hint: Include the remainder.)

   _____ days

3. There are 56 workers during each shift. The workers are split into teams of 14 each. How many teams work during a shift?

   _____ teams

4. Each shift, every workstation has an equal number of workers. Some workers are extras. How many extra workers are there?

   _____ workers

5. The plant hires 14 people just to work on Saturdays. This crew works a total of 98 hours one Saturday. If each person worked the same number of hours, how many hours did each person work?

   _____ hours

Lesson 3.4 Dividing 3 Digits by 2 Digits

Read the problem carefully and solve. Show your work under each question.

During summer vacation, many families take a trip by car. Several students at Milton Middle School talk about the trips they took last summer. They compare the distances and times they traveled.

Helpful Hint

To find the speed of a trip, divide the distance by the time.

For example, if you travel 220 miles in 11 hours, the speed is 20 miles per hour. (220 ÷ 11 = 20)

1. Ming's family drove 900 miles in 12 days. What was the average distance they drove each day?

   _____ miles

2. Alice's family drove a total of 495 miles in 11 hours. What was their average speed for the trip?

   _____ miles per hour

3. The Mendoza family drove 336 miles through national parks. It took them 14 hours to drive this distance. What was their average driving speed?

   _____ miles per hour

4. Jared's family drove on unpaved roads during part of their trip. It took them 15 hours to drive 315 miles. What was their average speed?

   _____ miles per hour

5. The Edwards family had car trouble on their vacation. It took them 27 hours to drive 135 miles. What was the average speed for this trip?

   _____ miles per hour

Lesson 3.5 Dividing 4 and 5 Digits by 2 Digits

Read the problem carefully and solve. Show your work under each question.

Athletes spend different amounts of times at practice. The number of hours that teams practice depends on the sport. Students at one school compared practice times for different sports.

Helpful Hint

To divide a 4-digit number by 2 digits, start with the 2 or 3 digits on the left of the dividend.

To divide 3,872 by 33, note that 33 is less than 38. Start by dividing 38 by 33.

To divide 3,872 by 53, note that 53 is more than 38. Start by dividing 387 by 53.

1. The total practice time for a football team is 4,380 hours. There are 73 players. How many hours does each player practice?

   _____ hours

2. A swim team has 31 swimmers. The total practice time for the team is 22,320 hours each season. How many hours per season does each swimmer practice?

   _____ hours

3. There are 18 players on the soccer team. They spend a total of 1,980 hours at practices and games. How many hours does each player spend at practices and games?

   _____ hours

4. A baseball team spends 3,267 hours in practice each season. There are 27 players on the team. How many hours does each player practice per season?

   _____ hours

Check What You Learned

Dividing through 5 Digits by 2 Digits

Read the problem carefully and solve. Show your work under each question.

Pyramid Products has a bonus plan at its plant. There are personal bonuses and team bonuses. Workers on teams usually split the team bonus equally.

1. A bonus of $156 is paid to one team of 3 workers. How much money does each person on the team get?

_____

2. Pyramid's manager pays $735 to a team of 12 workers. About how much money does each worker get?

about _____

3. One team of 21 workers splits a bonus of $1,995 equally. They each get the same amount of money. How much money does each worker get?

_____

4. Pyramid pays a $25 bonus for every good assembly idea. The company pays $2,950 this year. How many bonuses did Pyramid give this year?

_____ bonuses

5. Pyramid pays $10,330 in bonuses for new product ideas this year. A total of 93 workers receive these bonuses. Ninety-two people receive the same amount, and the last person receives the remainder.

Ninety-two people receive _____.

The last person receives _____.

Check What You Know

Understanding Fractions

Read the problem carefully and solve. Show your work under each question.

Tasty Cereal Company makes many kinds of breakfast foods. Tasty Cereal stores wheat, corn, and rice until they are used to make the food. Workers use fractions to show how much of each grain is left in storage. Workers use prime and composite numbers and factors in their jobs, too.

1. Alan looks for numbers to use that have more than two factors to label storage bins. His list includes 4, 6, 7, 8, 9, and 12. Which number is a prime number and only has two factors?

_____

2. Maria knows the sizes of the storage bins are multiples of common factors. One bin has 64 storage units and another has 48. What is the greatest common factor of 64 and 48?

_____

3. Sid needs to put 88 ounces of corn in 6 containers. Write $\frac{88}{6}$ as a mixed numeral.

_____

4. Another worker tells Keiko that the amount of wheat still in storage is $\frac{14}{49}$ of the original. Reduce this fraction to its simplest form.

_____

5. Roberto sees $\frac{42}{16}$ on a report. Write this improper fraction as a mixed numeral in the simplest form.

_____

6. Rosa reads that bins of rice are divided into equal groups. The result is $7\frac{5}{12}$. Write $7\frac{5}{12}$ as an improper fraction.

_____

Lesson 4.1 Numerator and Denominator

Read the problem carefully and solve. Show your work under each question.

Ms. Gordon owns a masonry business. Her company builds brick walls, sidewalks, and patios. Each day, she records how much work her workers complete on the job. She uses fractions to tell clients how much of the work is done. She also uses fractions to keep track of time.

Helpful Hint

The **numerator** is the number above the line of a fraction. The **denominator** is the number below the line of a fraction.

1. Ms. Gordon's workers have finished $\frac{7}{9}$ of a walk containing 1,800 bricks. What words would she say to express this fraction?

    _____

2. The shaded area of the diagram shows how much of a patio is complete. What fraction would the job manager use to describe the work that is complete?

    _____

3. Ms. Gordon told a client that a job would be done in seven days. Three days have passed. Write a fraction that shows three-sevenths of the time.

    _____ days

4. At the end of May, Ms. Gordon records how much of the year has gone by. She writes $\frac{5}{12}$. What is this fraction in words?

    _____

5. Recently, Ms. Gordon's company finished 5 of the 8 jobs that were in process. Shade part of the diagram to show the finished jobs as a fraction.

Lesson 4.2 Finding the Greatest Common Factor

Read the problem carefully and solve. Show your work under each question.

Ms. Boyce's science class is studying ants. She brings in some ant farms for the students to observe. The students have to keep track of the number of ants in each farm, since it changes often.

Helpful Hint

To find the **greatest common factor** for two or more numbers, list all of their factors. Then, look for the largest factor that is common to both.

1. Alberto counts the ants in two farms. One farm has 36 ants. The other has 54 ants. Find the greatest common factor of 36 and 54.

   _____

2. The two ant farms that Omar counts have 60 and 75 ants. What is the greatest common factor of 60 and 75?

   _____

3. Alma looks at two farms. One colony has 72 ants. Another has just 40 ants. What is the greatest common factor of 72 and 40?

   _____

4. Paula notices that one farm has 63 ants and another has 42 ants. What is the greatest common factor of 63 and 42?

   _____

5. Lana checks three farms. She sees a large difference in the number of ants in each one. What is the greatest common factor of 45, 72, and 99?

   _____

Lesson 4.3 Reducing Fractions to Their Simplest Form

Read the problem carefully and solve. Show your work under each question.

Sparkling Cookbook Company hires a cook to create some new recipes. The cook is good with recipe ideas, but not with math. The recipes have many complex fractions. The fractions must be reduced to their simplest forms.

Helpful Hint

To reduce a fraction, divide the top (numerator) and bottom (denominator) numbers by the same number.

1. One recipe for muffins calls for $\frac{22}{88}$ teaspoon of salt. What is the simplest form of the fraction?

_____ teaspoon

2. A new recipe for cookies requires $\frac{24}{72}$ cup of butter. What is this amount in its simplest form?

_____ cup

3. A soup recipe includes $\frac{17}{34}$ tablespoon of parsley. What is this fraction written in simplest form?

_____ tablespoon

4. A rice dish asks for $\frac{27}{36}$ cup of rice. What is the simplest form of this measurement?

_____ cup

5. A double recipe for custard needs $\frac{34}{51}$ cup of sugar. What is the simplest form of the fraction?

_____ cup

Lesson 4.4 Changing Improper Fractions to Mixed Numerals

Read the problem carefully and solve. Show your work under each question.

Carpenters solve math problems as they work. They saw boards into equal pieces. They divide lengths into equal parts. They need to know how to change improper fractions into mixed numerals.

Helpful Hint

In an **improper fraction**, the numerator is greater than the denominator. A **mixed numeral** is an improper fraction in its simplest form.

1. Frank has a board 66 inches long. He cuts it into 8 equal pieces. What is $\frac{66}{8}$ as a mixed numeral?

   _____ inches

2. Clara saws a board 32 inches long into 3 equal pieces. What is $\frac{32}{3}$ as a mixed numeral?

   _____ inches

3. Louis marks a wall with 6 equally spaced marks. The wall is 35 feet long. What mixed number is the same as $\frac{35}{6}$?

   _____ feet

4. Teresa measures a 32-foot board. She makes 5 marks at equal spaces on the board. What length is $\frac{32}{5}$ changed into a mixed numeral?

   _____ feet

5. Paul sets 8 fence posts in a line 60 feet long. What is the spacing of $\frac{60}{8}$ as a mixed number?

   _____ feet

Lesson 4.5 Working with Mixed Numerals

Read the problem carefully and solve. Show your work under each question.

Sometimes, carpenters work backward to check their math. They can turn mixed numerals back into improper fractions. If the improper fractions do not match the originals, the carpenters can look for errors.

Helpful Hint

To change a mixed numeral into an improper fraction, first multiply the whole number by the denominator. Then, add the numerator to the product.

To convert $2\frac{3}{8}$, multiply $2 \times 8 = 16$. Add $3 + 16 = 19$. The improper fraction is $\frac{19}{8}$.

1. Andre checks some marks he made to cut a board. The marks are each $6\frac{5}{8}$ inches apart. What is the length as an improper fraction?

   _____ inches

2. Patricia measures the distance between fence posts. Two posts are spaced $7\frac{3}{4}$ feet apart. What improper fraction shows this distance?

   _____ feet

3. Ruth sees a mixed numeral written as $9\frac{5}{10}$. How can Ruth write this number in its simplest form?

   _____

4. Colin checks some stakes he put in the ground. The stakes are $8\frac{1}{4}$ inches apart. What improper fraction would be equal to that space?

   _____ inches

5. Tony cuts a board into 6 equal parts. He measures the length as $5\frac{5}{16}$ inches. How should Tony write this length as an improper fraction?

   _____ inches

Check What You Learned

Understanding Fractions

Read the problem carefully and solve. Show your work under each question.

Jolly Balloon Shop keeps records of the different kinds of balloons it sells. It uses fractions to track which balloons sell best and factors to decide how many balloons to order.

1. Marcus notices the record of birthday balloons sold is the fraction $\frac{24}{32}$. Reduce the fraction to its simplest form.

   _____

2. One customer wants 25 red and 75 green balloons. Tanya has to order the right mix of balloons. Find the greatest common factor for the numbers 25 and 75.

   _____

3. Gilbert sees $\frac{84}{18}$ on a report from last week's sales. Write $\frac{84}{18}$ as a mixed numeral.

   _____

4. Sarah looks at a list of the numbers of balloons sold today: 4, 6, 8, 9, and 11. Which is a prime number?

   _____

5. Fourteen customers bought 36 baby balloons. Anna wrote the numbers as an improper fraction, $\frac{36}{14}$. Write the improper fraction as a mixed numeral in its simplest form.

   _____

6. Barbara writes a mixed number that shows how many more white balloons are sold than orange. Write $4\frac{13}{39}$ in its simplest form.

   _____

NAME _____

Check What You Know

Adding Fractions

Read the problem carefully and solve. Show your work under each question.

After people complete home projects, sometimes they have materials left over. Painting, cooking, and sewing projects often have leftover materials. A good way to make things neater around the house is to put the same kinds of leftover materials together.

1. Mr. Cooper has two cans with the same blue paint in his garage. He combines $\frac{1}{6}$ gallon with $\frac{1}{3}$ gallon. How much paint does he have?

   _____ gallon

2. Ms. Blanco has $\frac{1}{4}$ quart of cooking oil in one bottle and $\frac{1}{5}$ quart in another bottle. How much oil does she have when she combines the bottles?

   _____ quart

3. Inez made too much rice one evening. In one pan, she had $\frac{7}{10}$ pound. In another, she had $\frac{4}{5}$ pound. How much rice altogether did she have?

   _____ pounds

4. Amanda sees that there are two bags of flour on the shelf. One bag has $\frac{1}{8}$ pound and the other has $\frac{2}{5}$ pound. How much flour is on the shelf?

   _____ pound

5. Maria sews a dress. When she is done, she has $\frac{1}{16}$ yard and $\frac{3}{8}$ yard of fabric left over. How much extra fabric does she have in all?

   _____ yard

6. Burt has two bags of plant food. One bag has $\frac{5}{12}$ pound and the other has $\frac{1}{8}$ pound. How much plant food does Burt have in all?

   _____ pound

Lesson 5.1 Adding Fractions with Like Denominators

Read the problem carefully and solve. Show your work under each question.

Recipes use exact amounts of ingredients. Many recipes give the measurements of spices and other items in fractions. Common cooking measurements are teaspoons, tablespoons, and cups. Some recipes give measurements in ounces and pounds.

Helpful Hint

The sum of two fractions can be more than 1. If the sum is an improper fraction, change the fraction to a mixed numeral.

$$\frac{5}{7} + \frac{4}{7} = \frac{9}{7}$$

Then, $9 \div 7 = 1$ R 2. The mixed number is $1\frac{2}{7}$.

1. Mavis has a recipe for potato salad that uses $\frac{3}{4}$ cup of chopped onion and $\frac{3}{4}$ cup of water. How many cups of these two items are used?

   _____ cups

2. Patty is cooking dinner for her family. She makes a soup that uses $\frac{1}{3}$ teaspoon of paprika and $\frac{1}{3}$ teaspoon of garlic powder. How much paprika and garlic does she use?

   _____ teaspoon

3. Matt follows a recipe for rice that uses $\frac{1}{4}$ teaspoon of sage and $\frac{1}{4}$ teaspoon of basil. How many teaspoons of these two spices are used?

   _____ teaspoon

4. Emilio wants to be a chef. He makes a coffee cake that uses $\frac{2}{3}$ cup of coconut and $\frac{2}{3}$ cup of chocolate pieces. What is the total measurement of these two ingredients?

   _____ cups

5. Janet is making an egg dish. The recipe calls for $\frac{5}{8}$ cup of butter and $\frac{1}{8}$ cup of flour. How much butter and flour does the recipe use?

   _____ cup

Lesson 5.2 Finding Equivalent Fractions

Read the problem carefully and solve. Show your work under each question.

The weather station records the amount of rain and the amount of snow for a variety of cities. Some of the measurements are done in fractions. The record keepers have to find fractions with the same value. Fractions with the same value are equivalent fractions.

Helpful Hint

To convert a fraction into an equivalent fraction, multiply the top and bottom by the same nonzero number.

$$\frac{3}{4} \times \frac{5}{5} = \frac{15}{20}$$

1. Rainfall in Tucson one week was $\frac{4}{5}$ inch. What is an equivalent fraction with a denominator of 10?

   _____ inch

2. The snowfall in Denver one day was 3 inches. What is 3 inches written as a fraction with the denominator of 8?

   _____ inches

3. One day in Chicago, $\frac{2}{3}$ inch of rain was recorded. What fraction has the same value, but a denominator of 15?

   _____ inch

4. In Seattle, the rain one day was $\frac{1}{7}$ inch. What is an equivalent fraction with 21 for the denominator?

   _____ inch

5. The rainfall in New York one week was 2 inches. What is 2 inches written as a fraction with the denominator of 15?

   _____ inches

Lesson 5.3 Adding Fractions with Unlike Denominators

Read the problem carefully and solve. Show your work under each question.

In physical education class, students walk or run a certain distance. The teacher keeps track of the distance for each student.

Helpful Hint

When two fractions have different denominators, find the **least common multiple** (LCM) of the denominators. To add $\frac{1}{3} + \frac{1}{5}$, find the LCM of 3 and 5. The LCM is 15.

$$\frac{1}{3} \times \frac{5}{5} = \frac{5}{15}$$

$$\frac{1}{5} \times \frac{3}{3} = \frac{3}{15}$$

$$\frac{5}{15} + \frac{3}{15} = \frac{8}{15}$$

1. On Monday, Leon ran $\frac{1}{3}$ mile. On Wednesday, he walked $\frac{2}{5}$ mile in the time given. What total distance did he travel?

_____ mile

2. Tao walked $\frac{3}{8}$ mile today. Yesterday, she walked $\frac{2}{7}$ mile. What total distance did she walk?

_____ mile

3. Di walked $\frac{7}{10}$ mile last week and $\frac{1}{4}$ mile this week. How far did he walk in total?

_____ mile

4. Sejal ran $\frac{4}{9}$ mile today. Two days ago, she ran $\frac{3}{7}$ mile. What is the total distance she ran?

_____ mile

5. Naomi ran $\frac{3}{4}$ mile one day and walked $\frac{7}{8}$ mile a day later. What was her total distance?

_____ miles

NAME _____

Lesson 5.4 Adding Mixed Numerals with Unlike Denominators

Read the problem carefully and solve. Show your work under each question.

Camp Tonset has 4 hiking trails. The Pond Trail is $2\frac{3}{4}$ miles long, the Willow Trail is $1\frac{1}{2}$ miles long, the Birch Trail is $6\frac{3}{5}$ miles long, and the Cliff Trail is $5\frac{1}{3}$ miles long.

Helpful Hint

Remember to find a common denominator and rename the fractions before you add.

Make sure to write each answer in simplest form.

1. Catherine hikes the Pond Trail and the Willow Trail. How many miles does she hike in all?

_____ miles

2. Before she left camp, Catherine also hiked the Cliff Trail. How many total miles did she hike?

_____ miles

3. Marco hiked the Birch Trail and the Willow Trail at the same camp. Who hiked the most miles, Marco or Catherine?

_____ hiked the most miles.

4. Next summer, Catherine wants to hike 2 trails, the one trail she did not hike this year and her favorite, the Pond Trail. How far altogether will she hike on those two trails?

_____ miles

5. Ariana plans to hike the Cliff Trail and the Willow Trail next summer. How far altogether will she hike?

_____ miles

Check What You Learned

Adding Fractions

Read the problem carefully and solve. Show your work under each question.

The Good-to-Go Shop sells foods that are ready to eat. The shop sells many types of foods, including sandwiches, salads, desserts, and drinks. Customers can buy most foods in fractions.

1. Hana likes salads. She buys $\frac{1}{4}$ pound of one salad and $\frac{3}{16}$ pound of another. How many pounds of salad does she buy in all?

_____ pound

2. Mr. Ahn buys relishes for a lunch party. He buys $\frac{7}{8}$ pound of pickles and $\frac{9}{10}$ pound of olives. How much altogether do these foods weigh?

_____ pounds

3. Beatriz buys two kinds of sushi. She buys $\frac{1}{3}$ pound of each. How much does all the sushi weigh?

_____ pound

4. Rama buys a drink for herself and a friend. The first is $\frac{3}{8}$ quart and the second is $\frac{5}{8}$ quart. How many quarts did she buy in all?

_____ quart

5. Pasta salad costs $2.00 for $\frac{1}{4}$ pound. Percy finds a fraction with the same value. What is an equivalent fraction with a denominator of 12?

_____ pound

6. Tony buys some potato salad. He buys $\frac{9}{11}$ pound. Later, he buys $\frac{7}{8}$ pound. How much potato salad did he buy in total?

_____ pounds

NAME _____

Check What You Know

Subtracting Fractions and Understanding Decimals

Read the problem carefully and solve. Show your work under each question.

People spend a lot of time watching TV, videos, and movies. They also spend a lot of time reading information on the Internet. The time people spend on these activities can be described as fractions of time units.

1. Farha surfed the Internet for $\frac{8}{9}$ hour on Monday. The next day, she was online for $\frac{1}{9}$ hour. What is the difference between these two amounts of time?

   _____ hour

2. Last month, Chou watched a movie that was $2\frac{5}{8}$ hours long. Yesterday, he watched a movie that was $1\frac{7}{8}$ hours long. How much longer was the movie he watched last month?

   _____ hour

3. Trina watched TV for 3 hours on Sunday. On Monday, she watched TV for $\frac{2}{5}$ hour. How much longer did she watch TV on Sunday than on Monday?

   _____ hours

4. Nancy watches a video for 0.25 hour in the morning. At night, she watches the same video for 0.875 hour. How much longer did she watch the video at night?

   _____ hour

5. Scott spent $4\frac{5}{6}$ hours watching a history program. He spent $2\frac{1}{6}$ hours doing homework on the computer. What is the difference between these two amounts of time?

   _____ hours

6. Kento spends 8.3 hours a week watching TV and 6.5 hours a week practicing the piano. Each week, how much more time does he spend watching TV?

   _____ hours

Lesson 6.1 Subtracting Fractions with Like Denominators

Read the problem carefully and solve. Show your work under each question.

Grocery stores arrange food and other products on shelves to attract customers to buy the products. The stores give more space to products with a high profit. Managers also place products in very visible spots to catch the eyes of impulse buyers.

Helpful Hint

Like fractions have the same denominator. $\frac{1}{4}$ and $\frac{3}{4}$ have like denominators. To subtract fractions with like denominators, subtract the numerators. The denominator stays the same. Remember to simplify the answer.

1. About $\frac{4}{5}$ of the food on the shelves at Top Foods are packaged. $\frac{1}{5}$ of the food in the store are vegetables and fruit. What is the difference between the amounts of packaged food and the vegetables and fruit?

   _____

2. In Speedy Mart, $\frac{5}{6}$ of the foods sold are for eating immediately. $\frac{1}{6}$ of the foods sold can be stored. What is the difference between the amounts of the two types of food?

   _____

3. In a cleaning products section, $\frac{5}{8}$ of the products are for clothes and $\frac{3}{8}$ are for other uses. What is the difference between the amounts of these products?

   _____

4. Cora shelves soups at the store. She sees that $\frac{6}{7}$ of the soups are regular and $\frac{1}{7}$ are premium. How much more of the soups are regular than premium?

   _____

5. Alejandro puts drinks in the refrigerators. $\frac{7}{9}$ of the drinks are milk. $\frac{2}{9}$ of the drinks are juices. How much more milk products are there than juices?

   _____

Lesson 6.2 Subtracting Fractions from Whole Numbers

Read the problem carefully and solve. Show your work under each question.

The Delgado family visits relatives in five different towns. Mr. Delgado makes a game of the travel time going from town to town. He asks his three children to figure out how much time is left on each leg of the trip.

Helpful Hint

To subtract a fraction from a whole number, change the whole number to a mixed numeral. To subtract $\frac{1}{5}$ from 2, change 2 to $1\frac{5}{5}$. Then, subtract $\frac{1}{5}$ to get $\frac{4}{5}$.

1. It takes 7 hours to go from Vista to Pineville. After driving for $\frac{2}{3}$ hour, Mr. Delgado asks Ricardo to find the time remaining. How much time is left before they get to Pineville?

   _____hours

2. The drive from Pineville to Tucker takes 5 hours. After driving for $\frac{5}{9}$ hour, Felice figures the time left. How much longer will they travel?

   _____hours

3. From Tucker to Sparta, the drive takes 3 hours. After the family travels for $\frac{7}{15}$ hour, Luz figures the time left. How much longer will the trip take?

   _____ hours

4. The trip from Sparta to Norwood lasts for 4 hours. When the family has gone for $\frac{5}{12}$ hour, Ricardo finds the time left. What is it?

   _____ hours

5. The trip from Norwood back to Vista takes 8 hours. When the Delgados are $\frac{2}{3}$ hour from Vista, how many hours have they driven?

   _____ hours

Lesson 6.3 Subtracting Mixed Numerals with Like Denominators

Read the problem carefully and solve. Show your work under each question.

The Starters Bicycle Club sponsors rides for new riders. The rides are marked on a map and graded from easy to challenging. Checkpoints on the rides help riders to know how far they have gone.

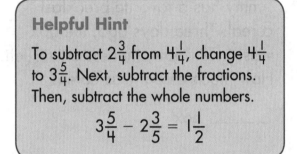

Helpful Hint

To subtract $2\frac{3}{4}$ from $4\frac{1}{4}$, change $4\frac{1}{4}$ to $3\frac{5}{4}$. Next, subtract the fractions. Then, subtract the whole numbers.

$$3\frac{5}{4} - 2\frac{3}{5} = 1\frac{1}{2}$$

1. Aaron is riding with the club for the first time. The ride is $6\frac{5}{8}$ miles. When Aaron has gone $3\frac{1}{8}$ miles, how much farther does he have to go?

   _____ miles

2. Kuri is riding $5\frac{3}{7}$ miles today. She has ridden $1\frac{2}{7}$ miles already. How many miles are left?

   _____ miles

3. Beth has ridden $2\frac{7}{12}$ miles of an $8\frac{3}{12}$-mile ride. How many miles are left?

   _____ miles

4. Three riders are going up a $2\frac{5}{9}$-mile hill. They have gone $1\frac{2}{9}$ miles so far. How many miles are left?

   _____ miles

5. Bill rode $9\frac{5}{11}$ miles last week. This week he rode $5\frac{9}{11}$ miles. What is the difference in the two distances?

   _____ miles

Lesson 6.4 Subtracting Fractions with Unlike Denominators

Read the problem carefully and solve. Show your work under each question.

Ms. Sakata teaches a class on living skills. She tells students that they can use fractions in everyday life. Fractions can describe how much of a household product is used. Fractions can also describe how much of a product remains.

Helpful Hint

To subtract fractions with unlike denominators, change them to fractions with like denominators.

To solve $\frac{3}{4} - \frac{2}{5}$, multiply $\frac{3}{4} \times \frac{5}{5} = \frac{15}{20}$ and multiply $\frac{2}{5} \times \frac{4}{4} = \frac{8}{20}$.

Then, $\frac{15}{20} - \frac{8}{20} = \frac{7}{20}$.

1. Kaya notices that the kitchen cleanser can is $\frac{1}{5}$ full. Two weeks ago, it was $\frac{2}{3}$ full. How much cleanser was used?

_____ can

2. Masako's sisters used his shampoo. A week ago, the bottle was $\frac{7}{8}$ full. Now, only $\frac{1}{6}$ is left. How much shampoo was used?

_____ bottle

3. Jimmy has a favorite breakfast cereal. Three days ago, the box was $\frac{3}{5}$ full. Now, there is only $\frac{1}{6}$ left. How much cereal was eaten?

_____ box

4. Camila likes orange juice. Today, the carton is $\frac{1}{7}$ full. Yesterday, it was $\frac{3}{5}$ full. How much orange juice did Camila's family drink?

_____ carton

5. Tara notices the sack of potatoes has $\frac{1}{8}$ of the potatoes left. Two weeks ago, the sack was $\frac{7}{9}$ full. How much of the sack of potatoes was used?

_____ sack

Spectrum Word Problems
Grade 5
38

Lesson 6.4
Subtracting Fractions with Unlike Denominators

Lesson 6.5 Subtracting Mixed Numerals with Unlike Denominators

Read the problem carefully and solve. Show your work under each question.

Students at Mercerville High School study how to manage their money. They keep records of how much fuel they buy for their cars. They want to see who is getting the best mileage each week.

Helpful Hint

To subtract mixed numerals, first change unlike fractions to have like denominators. You might have to make one of the fractions into an improper fraction. Then, subtract the fractions. Finally, subtract the whole numbers.

1. Carl bought $7\frac{3}{10}$ gallons of gas last week. Today, he has $2\frac{4}{5}$ gallons left. How much gas did he use?

   _____ gallons

2. Yesterday, Kendra bought $8\frac{2}{3}$ gallons of fuel. Today, she has $7\frac{1}{6}$ gallons left. How much fuel did she use?

   _____ gallons

3. Two days ago, Nate put $6\frac{2}{7}$ gallons of gas in his tank. Today, he has $5\frac{4}{9}$ gallons left. How much gas did Nate use?

   _____ gallon

4. Donna bought $9\frac{1}{2}$ gallons of fuel. She used $7\frac{2}{3}$ gallons. How much fuel does she have left?

   _____ gallons

5. Rosa took a trip this week. She had $9\frac{3}{11}$ gallons of gas when she started. When she got home, she had $1\frac{4}{7}$ gallons left. How much did she use?

   _____ gallons

Lesson 6.6 Understanding Decimals

Read the problem carefully and solve. Show your work under each question.

Rob's class grew plants in their science class. Each student planted a few seeds in a pot. They kept track of their plant's height each day. One day, the students decided to compare the heights of their plants.

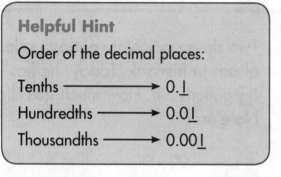

Helpful Hint

Order of the decimal places:

Tenths ⟶ 0.1

Hundredths ⟶ 0.01

Thousandths ⟶ 0.001

1. Jen's plant is 13.47 centimeters tall. Which digit is in the hundredths place?

    _____

2. Alex's plant is 14.623 centimeters tall. Which digit is in the thousandths place?

    _____

3. Ada's plant is 8.14 centimeters tall. Dan's plant is 8.41 centimeters tall. Compare the two decimals using <, >, or =.

    _____

4. Pam had to change her plant's measurements from centimeters to meters. She calculated her plant was 0.089 meter. Which digit is in the thousandths place?

    _____

Lesson 6.7 Rounding Decimals

Read the problem carefully and solve. Show your work under each question.

Frank finds rounding helpful when doing errands.

Helpful Hint

To round a decimal to a designated place value, first underline that place. If the digit to the right is 5 through 9, round up. If the digit to the right is 1 through 4, round down, leave the digit in the designated place unchanged, and drop all digits to the right.

1. Frank put 5.1436 gallons of gasoline in his car. What is 5.1436 rounded to the nearest hundredth?

   _____

2. Frank went to lunch with his friend, Kevin. Frank's lunch was $8.21 and Kevin's lunch was $7.16. What was the total cost to the nearest tenth?

   _____

3. At the grocery store, Frank weighed some apples. They weighed 10.508 pounds. He put back 6.1 pounds. Estimate the difference by rounding each number to the nearest whole number, and then subtract.

   _____

4. Frank wants to buy 3 items that cost $6.68, $5.83, and $10.21. Estimate the sum by rounding each number to the nearest whole number, and then adding.

   _____

5. The distance from the grocery store to Frank's house is 4.236 miles. What is 4.236 rounded to the nearest tenth?

   _____

Lesson 6.8 Adding and Subtracting Decimals

Read the problem carefully and solve. Show your work under each question.

Pedro researches the amount of snowfall in a mountain town that is popular for skiing. The amount of snow measured last November was 21.23 inches. In December, the snowfall was 25.67 inches, and in January it was 24.78 inches. In February, the snowfall measured 22.17 inches.

Helpful Hint

To add and subtract decimals:

1. Line up the decimal points.
2. Add or subtract like you would whole numbers.
3. Make sure to include the decimal point in the correct place in your answer.

1. Pedro compares the snowfall amounts in December and January. What is the difference between the two amounts?

   _____ in.

3. Pedro learned that the total snowfall for the same four months the year before was 101.34 inches. How much more snow fell that year?

   _____ in.

4. How much more snow fell in December than in February?

   _____ in.

2. What was the total snowfall amount for all four months?

   _____ in.

5. What is the difference between the amount of snow measured in January and February?

   _____ in.

Lesson 6.9 Multiplying and Dividing Decimals

Read the problem carefully and solve. Show your work under each question.

Julie is buying supplies and decorations for Halloween.

1. Boxes of orange and purple lights are 3 for $15.90. What is the cost of one box?

_____

2. Halloween cards come in boxes of 6 for $14.33, 8 for $16.12, or 10 for $17.42. Which is the best deal?

_____

3. Candy corn costs $8.76 per pound. How much does 9 pounds of candy corn cost?

_____

4. A factory makes 7.34 kilograms of pumpkin pie filling per minute. How many kilograms will they make in 24 minutes?

_____ kg

5. Each bag contains 12.78 ounces of chocolate. If Julie buys 11 bags, how many ounces of chocolate will she get altogether?

_____ oz

6. Julie buys 12 packages of Halloween stickers for $14.40. How much does one package of Halloween stickers cost?

_____

Check What You Learned

Subtracting Fractions

Read the problem carefully and solve. Show your work under each question.

Each person has unique features. Differing features include personality, interests, and skills. Differing features also include age, height, and other physical features. Some differing features can be expressed as fractions.

1. Carlota is $5\frac{1}{12}$ feet tall. Her sister is $5\frac{5}{12}$ feet tall. What is the difference between their heights?

   _____ foot

2. Chung's hat measures 6.375 units. His friend's hat measures 6.75 units. What is the difference in the hat sizes?

   _____ units

3. Lourdes is 8 years old. Her little sister is $\frac{5}{7}$ of a year old. What is the difference between their ages?

   _____ years

4. Roger can walk a mile in $\frac{1}{3}$ hour. His twin brother can walk the same distance in $\frac{3}{10}$ hour. What is the difference between the two amounts of time?

   _____ hour

5. Mari is $8\frac{5}{6}$ years old. Her neighbor is $9\frac{3}{5}$ years old. How much older than Mari is her neighbor?

   _____ year

6. Tracy has spent $\frac{1}{7}$ of her years in school. Gina has spent $\frac{3}{14}$ of her years in school. What is the difference between these amounts of time?

   _____ year

Mid-Test Chapters 1-6

Read the problem carefully and solve. Show your work under each question.

Wheat is one of the main food crops that farmers grow. The wheat harvest in the U.S. is over 2 billion bushels yearly. Some states grow a lot of wheat and others grow only a small amount. The harvest is measured in units of 1,000 bushels.

---

1. One year, farmers in Florida harvested 513 units of wheat. The farmers in West Virginia harvested 348 units. What is the difference between the number of units?

_____ units

2. Recently, the wheat harvest in New Mexico was 1,428 units. The harvest in Missouri was 37,840 units. What is the total number of units?

_____ units

3. Farmers in Washington harvested 128,722 units of wheat. The wheat harvest in Idaho was 83,675 units. How many more units of wheat were harvested in Washington than in Idaho?

_____ units

4. In Arizona, 8,260 units of wheat were harvested. In Illinois, the harvest was 50,730 units. Estimate the sum of these two wheat harvests.

about _____ units

5. Farmers in South Dakota harvested 147,516 units of wheat. Farmers in California harvested 28,700 units of wheat. What is the difference between the two harvests?

_____ units

6. Kansas produced 283,000 units. North Dakota produced 300,050 units. Montana produced 149,820 units. How many total units of wheat were produced in these three states?

_____ units

Mid-Test Chapters 1–6

Read the problem carefully and solve. Show your work under each question.

The Speedy Bicycle Company makes parts for other bicycle factories. Speedy also sells parts to bike shops. The company makes some bike parts when customers ask for the parts. Speedy ships the parts directly to its customers.

1. Seven factories ordered sets of bicycle spokes. Speedy has 1,354 sets of spokes in stock. If the same number of sets are shipped to each factory, how many sets does each factory get? How many sets are left over?

_____ sets

_____ sets left over

2. Speedy makes bike seats when orders arrive. Nine factories each ordered 162 seats. How many seats does Speedy have to make?

_____ seats

3. Laura buys boxes to pack the bike parts. There are 113 crates and each crate holds 135 boxes. How many boxes does Laura buy?

_____ boxes

4. Alec packs reflectors in boxes. Each box holds 48 reflectors. Alec has 828 reflectors to ship. How many boxes will Alec fill? How many reflectors will be left over?

_____ boxes

_____ reflectors left over

5. Steve ships boxes of bolts. Each box holds 38 bolts. He shipped 1,288 boxes this year. How many bolts altogether did he ship this year?

_____ bolts

6. Speedy made 24,150 sprockets last year. They sold them to 23 customers who each bought the same number of sprockets. How many sprockets did each customer buy?

_____ sprockets

Mid-Test Chapters 1–6

Read the problem carefully and solve. Show your work under each question.

The Bright Blooms Florist Shop makes and delivers flower bouquets to customers in the city. The shop has many kinds and colors of flowers in stock. Staff members use fractions to keep track of the flowers in the store. They also use prime and composite numbers.

1. Betty counts the number of bunches of blue flowers sold by the end of the week. The shop sold $\frac{18}{24}$ of the blue flowers. What is this fraction written in its simplest form?

   _____

2. Rudy finds out that sunflowers are $4\frac{3}{7}$ more popular than lilies. Write $4\frac{3}{7}$ as an improper fraction.

   _____

3. Sally writes the ratio $\frac{47}{15}$ to compare the sales of roses for two weeks. Write $\frac{47}{15}$ as a mixed numeral.

   _____

4. One weekend, 32 bridal bouquets are ordered. 54 bouquets are ordered for the next weekend. Irene needs to find the greatest common factor for these numbers. What is the greatest common factor?

   _____

5. Ms. Foster, the store owner, looks at a list of numbers of flower orders. The list is 2, 3, 5, 7, 9, and 11. She notices one number is a composite number. Which is a composite number?

   _____

6. Ms. Foster reads that customers buy $3\frac{5}{8}$ times as many roses as daisies. Write $3\frac{5}{8}$ as an improper fraction.

   _____

Mid-Test Chapters 1–6

Read the problem carefully and solve. Show your work under each question.

The town of Tyler has a park cleanup week once a year. The town asks students from the schools to help clean up the parks in their neighborhoods. Parents and students work together to get rid of trash and do other chores to make the parks look better.

1. The Sakatas pull weeds at a playground. They work 4.6 hours for 3 days. How many hours altogether do they work?

_____ hours

2. At Moss Park, students work a total of $3\frac{7}{8}$ days. At Piney Park, students work a total of $2\frac{3}{8}$ days. How many more days did students work at Moss Park than at Piney Park?

_____ days

3. At Nova Park, the Carter family works for 5 hours, and a neighbor works for $\frac{5}{6}$ hour. How many total hours were worked at Nova Park?

_____ hours

4. In Benson Park, workers clear 1.6 acres of trash in an hour. At Alto Park, workers clear 1.7 acres in an hour. What total area is cleared in one hour?

_____ acres

5. Pedro paints 3 trash cans. His little brother paints $\frac{1}{2}$ trash can. How many more trash cans does Pedro paint than his little brother?

_____ trash cans

6. At DeSoto Park, workers plant $8\frac{1}{6}$ square yards of flowers. At Kramer Park, they plant $6\frac{3}{4}$ square yards. What is the difference?

_____ square yards

Check What You Know

Multiplying Fractions

Read the problem carefully and solve. Show your work under each question.

Jolly Island Amusement Park has many rides and activities. Visitors can stay for just a few hours, or they can stay all day.

1. The pathways in the park have a total distance of $2\frac{1}{3}$ miles. Claire walks $\frac{3}{8}$ of the total distance. How many miles has she walked?

_____ mile

2. At the park, giant sandwiches each weigh $\frac{5}{7}$ pound. Samuel and 6 friends each eat a giant sandwich. What is the total weight of the sandwiches they ate?

_____ pounds

3. Visitors spend $\frac{1}{3}$ of their time waiting in lines for rides. If the Santos family spends $5\frac{3}{4}$ hours at the park, how long do they wait in lines?

_____ hours

4. Cotton candy weighs $\frac{1}{8}$ pound. Eartha eats $\frac{3}{5}$ of her cotton candy. What is the weight of the cotton candy she ate?

_____ pound

5. Anita spends $6\frac{4}{5}$ hours at the park. She plans to spend $2\frac{1}{2}$ times as many hours on her next visit. How many hours will she spend at the park on her next visit?

_____ hours

6. Francisco and 5 friends ride the longest roller coaster at the park, which takes $3\frac{5}{6}$ minutes. What is the total combined time they spend on the coaster?

_____ minutes

Lesson 7.1 Multiplying Mixed Numerals and Whole Numbers

Read the problem carefully and solve. Show your work under each question.

At Oak Forest Camp, the cook keeps records to show how much food the campers eat. Most of the records are ordinary. A few of the young campers try to set records for how much they eat.

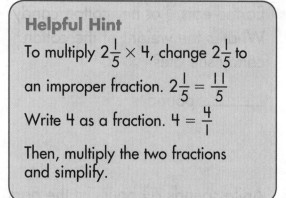

Helpful Hint

To multiply $2\frac{1}{5} \times 4$, change $2\frac{1}{5}$ to an improper fraction. $2\frac{1}{5} = \frac{11}{5}$

Write 4 as a fraction. $4 = \frac{4}{1}$

Then, multiply the two fractions and simplify.

1. Each of three boys eats a stack of pancakes $4\frac{1}{4}$ inches tall. How tall is a stack of all these pancakes?

_____ inches

2. Four campers each ate $8\frac{1}{2}$ slices of toast one morning. How many slices of toast altogether did they eat?

_____ slices

3. Eleven girls each ate $1\frac{1}{3}$ apples per day. How many apples did they eat each day in total?

_____ apples

4. The cook asks 8 campers for help slicing melons. Each camper slices $3\frac{1}{4}$ melons. How many melons do they slice in total?

_____ melons

5. Nine campers each eat $7\frac{2}{3}$ cups of strawberries. What is the total number of cups of strawberries they eat?

_____ cups

Lesson 7.2 Multiplying Mixed Numerals

Read the problem carefully and solve. Show your work under each question.

The fees of freight companies are based on the distance that things are shipped. Freight companies promise to deliver in a certain amount of time. The shipping times depend on the distance shipped.

Helpful Hint

To multiply two mixed numerals, first change each one into an improper fraction. Then, multiply the fractions and reduce to the simplest form.

1. Speedy Deliveries takes $3\frac{1}{5}$ hours to ship a desk 100 miles. How long would it take to ship the same desk $4\frac{1}{2}$ times as far?

   _____ hours

2. Slow Time Trucking needs $5\frac{1}{2}$ hours to move a shipment 15 miles. How long would it take to move the same shipment $1\frac{3}{4}$ times as far?

   _____ hours

3. It takes $2\frac{1}{3}$ hours for Quicksilver Movers to move a load of boxes 70 miles. How long would it take to move the boxes $2\frac{1}{5}$ times as far?

   _____ hours

4. In $4\frac{2}{3}$ hours, Jet Trucking moves a load of barrels 120 miles. How long would it take to move the barrels a distance that is $3\frac{1}{3}$ times as far?

   _____ hours

5. Cautious Shippers moves a load of furniture 6 miles in $1\frac{1}{8}$ hours. How long would it take to move the furniture $2\frac{1}{3}$ times farther?

   _____ hours

Lesson 7.3 Multiplying Fractions

Read the problem carefully and solve. Show your work under each question. Reduce your answer to simplest form.

Miguel and Sean have a lawn mowing service in their neighborhood. To find the area of a lawn, or a rectangle, multiply the length times the width.

$$\text{area} = \text{length} \times \text{width}$$
$$= 4\frac{2}{7} \times 6\frac{3}{8}$$
$$= 27\frac{9}{28}$$

$6\frac{3}{8}$

$4\frac{2}{7}$

Helpful Hint

To multiply two fractions, first multiply the numerators. Then, multiply the denominators. Finally, reduce the fraction to the simplest form.

1. Miguel stops for a break after he mows $\frac{4}{5}$ of the Andersons' lawn. The lawn measures $\frac{7}{8}$ acre. How much of the lawn did Miguel mow?

_____ acre

2. The Chang lawn measures $31\frac{2}{3}$ yards by $33\frac{3}{7}$ yards. What is the area of the lawn?

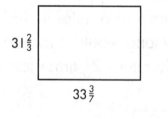

$31\frac{2}{3}$

$33\frac{3}{7}$

_____ acres

3. The Williams home has a lawn that measures $\frac{3}{11}$ acre. After Miguel mows $\frac{5}{6}$ of the lawn, it begins to rain, and he can't finish the job. How much of the lawn has he mowed?

_____ acre

4. Miguel mows $\frac{3}{10}$ of the Rivera lawn, and Sean mows the rest. The lawn measures $\frac{7}{12}$ acre. How much of the lawn did Miguel mow?

_____ acre

5. The lawn at the Jacobs' home measures $23\frac{4}{9}$ yards by $25\frac{3}{8}$ yards. What is the area of the lawn?

_____ acres

Check What You Learned

Multiplying Fractions

Read the problem carefully and solve. Show your work under each question.

Many cities have tour buses that take visitors to see the sights. The Elegant City Tour Company takes people to famous spots. The tour buses also stop to let visitors walk around and shop.

1. A short tour is $10\frac{1}{3}$ miles. When the tour bus has driven $\frac{3}{8}$ of the tour, how many miles has it gone?

   _____ miles

2. On one bus, $\frac{7}{9}$ of the people said they want to take the tour again. If there are 18 people on the bus, how many want to take the tour again?

   _____ people

3. One tour lasts $2\frac{5}{6}$ hours. Nine people take the tour. How many total hours do they spend on the tour?

   _____ hours

4. When the bus stopped at a shopping area, 6 visitors each walked $\frac{3}{5}$ mile. What total distance did they walk?

   _____ miles

5. A long tour lasts $4\frac{1}{5}$ hours. When the tour is $\frac{5}{8}$ complete, how long have people been on the tour?

   _____ hours

6. At the end of a $3\frac{3}{4}$-hour tour, one visitor said he wished the tour had been $1\frac{1}{2}$ times as long. How many hours would that have been?

   _____ hours

Check What You Know

Dividing Fractions

Read the problem carefully and solve. Show your work under each question.

The Hernandez family has a birthday party for one of their children. They invite friends from the neighborhood and family. At the party, they serve a meal for all of the guests.

---

1. Mrs. Hernandez slices sandwiches into equal parts. There are 5 sandwiches, and each slice $\frac{1}{8}$ of a sandwich. How many slices of sandwiches are there?

_____ slices

2. $\frac{5}{6}$ of one sandwich is left. 5 people want to divide the sandwich equally. How much does each person get?

_____ of the sandwich

3. Mr. Hernandez bought $8\frac{1}{3}$ liters of soda to drink. This total was $1\frac{3}{4}$ times more soda than the guests drank. How many liters of the soda did the guests drink?

_____ liters

4. There are 4 quarts of ice cream for the party. Each serving is $\frac{1}{7}$ quart. How many servings of ice cream are there?

_____ servings

5. Mr. Hernandez cuts a sheet cake into equal pieces. Two pieces are left. These are $\frac{1}{16}$ of the cake. Into how many pieces was the cake cut?

_____ pieces

6. Mrs. Hernandez buys $2\frac{1}{5}$ ounces of candy. If each guest gets $\frac{1}{6}$ of the candy, how many ounces of candy does each guest get?

_____ ounces

Lesson 8.1 Reciprocals and Dividing Whole Numbers and Fractions

Read the problem carefully and solve. Show your work under each question.

Milestone Middle School has a student band. The musicians practice together and at home. It takes several hours of practice each week for students to learn the music and play it well.

Helpful Hint

To divide a whole number by a fraction, first rewrite the fraction as its reciprocal. Then, multiply the whole number by the reciprocal.

1. The Milestone band practices twice a week at school. The total practice time is $4\frac{5}{7}$ hours. Each session is equal in length. How many hours long is each practice session?

   _____ hours

2. Mr. Davis asks his students questions that link music to math. He asks, "What is the reciprocal of $\frac{3}{4}$ time?"

   _____

3. Melvin practices a total of $6\frac{2}{3}$ hours in three days. If he practices for the same amount of time each day, how many hours does he practice each day?

   _____ hours

4. Charlene practices 4 days a week for a total of $7\frac{3}{5}$ hours. She practices for the same amount of time each day. How many hours does she practice each day?

   _____ hours

5. Four musicians represent $\frac{1}{8}$ of the band members. How many musicians are in the band?

   _____ musicians

Lesson 8.2 Dividing Fractions by Fractions

Read the problem carefully and solve. Show your work under each question.

Recipes in cookbooks give directions to make different types of food. Most recipes tell how many servings the recipe makes. If a recipe does not make enough to serve everyone, the cook has to increase the ingredient amounts.

Helpful Hint

To divide a simple fraction by a fraction, change the second fraction to a reciprocal. Then, multiply the first fraction by the reciprocal.

$$\frac{2}{3} \div \frac{4}{5} = \frac{2}{3} \times \frac{5}{4} = \frac{5}{6}$$

1. Mr. Kwan has a recipe that takes $\frac{3}{8}$ cup of broth. This recipe is enough for $\frac{1}{2}$ of what Mr. Kwan wants. How much broth does he need?

_____ cup

2. Thelma has a recipe that takes $\frac{3}{5}$ teaspoon of lemon juice. This recipe makes $\frac{1}{6}$ of the cookies that Thelma wants. How much lemon juice does she need to make all the cookies?

_____ teaspoon

3. A recipe for stuffed peppers takes $\frac{1}{6}$ teaspoon of garlic salt. The recipe makes $\frac{1}{4}$ of the amount of peppers Ms. Santos needs. How much garlic salt will she use to make all the peppers she needs?

_____ teaspoon

4. Nolan has a recipe that makes $\frac{1}{12}$ of the amount he wants. The recipe takes $\frac{7}{9}$ cup of egg whites. How many total cups of egg whites will he need to make the total amount?

_____ cups

5. Robyn has a pasta recipe that takes $\frac{5}{7}$ pound of cheese. It makes $\frac{1}{11}$ of the amount she needs. How much cheese does she need in total?

_____ pounds

Lesson 8.3 Dividing Mixed Numerals

Read the problem carefully and solve. Show your work under each question.

Often, actions are described by how long they take to complete. *Miles per hour*, for example, describes how many miles are traveled in one hour.

Helpful Hint

To divide a mixed numeral by a mixed numeral, change both to improper fractions. Rewrite the fraction you are dividing by as its reciprocal. Then, multiply the first fraction by the reciprocal.

$$2\frac{1}{3} \div 1\frac{5}{6} = \frac{7}{3} \div \frac{11}{6} = \frac{7}{3} \times \frac{6}{11} = \frac{14}{11} = 1\frac{3}{11}$$

1. A crew of painters finished $4\frac{4}{5}$ rooms in 3 hours. If they paint the same amount each hour, how many rooms did they paint in one hour?

_____ rooms per hour

2. In one soccer league, 4 teams played $2\frac{1}{2}$ games in $5\frac{1}{6}$ hours. Each game lasted the same amount of time. What fraction of a game was played in 1 hour?

_____ game per hour

3. In a wooded area, tree cutters cut down $1\frac{1}{9}$ acres of trees in 3 weeks. If they cut the same number of acres each week, how many acres did they cut per week?

_____ acre per week

4. Eight roofers installed $3\frac{3}{7}$ roofs in one week. If all the workers completed equal amounts of work, what amount of the roof did each one install?

_____ roof per worker

5. In a computer game, 5 towns were built in $6\frac{1}{5}$ hours. If the towns were built at the same rate, what fraction of a town was built in 1 hour?

_____ town per hour

Lesson 8.4 Fractions and Line Plots

Read the problem carefully and solve. Show your work under each question.

Mr. Weber's class measured different amounts of water into 12 beakers for an experiment. The amount of water in each beaker is below.

$\frac{1}{4}$ cup, $\frac{1}{4}$ cup, $\frac{1}{2}$ cup, $\frac{3}{4}$ cup, $\frac{1}{4}$ cup, $\frac{1}{4}$ cup, $\frac{1}{4}$ cup, $\frac{1}{2}$ cup, $\frac{1}{4}$ cup, $\frac{3}{4}$ cup, $\frac{1}{4}$ cup, $\frac{3}{4}$ cup

---

1. Count the number of cups for each amount.

    $\frac{1}{4}$: _____

    $\frac{1}{2}$: _____

    $\frac{3}{4}$: _____

    Draw an × for the number of times each amount is recorded to complete the line plot.

    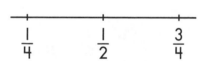

    Water used (in cups)

2. What is the total amount of water in all the beakers that contain $\frac{1}{4}$ cup water?

    _____ cups

3. What is the total amount of water in all the beakers that contain $\frac{1}{2}$ cup water?

    _____ cup

4. Find the total amount of water in all of the beakers that contain $\frac{3}{4}$ cup of water.

    _____ cups

5. What is the total amount of water in all the beakers?

    _____ cups

6. What is the average amount of water in a beaker?

    _____ cups

Check What You Learned

Dividing Fractions

Read the problem carefully and solve. Show your work under each question.

The bride's family hires a caterer to provide food for a wedding reception. The caterer knows how many people are invited to the reception and decides how much food to prepare.

1. The caterer mixes $4\frac{1}{4}$ gallons of lemon punch. It is $1\frac{3}{8}$ times as much as the guests drink. How much punch do the guests drink?

   _____ gallons

2. A full dinner is served at the reception. Four guests do not stay for dinner. This is $\frac{1}{12}$ of the total number of guests. How many guests attend the reception in total?

   _____ guests

3. During dinner, six guests drink a total of $\frac{3}{8}$ gallon of fizzy apple juice. If each guest drinks the same amount, how many gallons of fizzy apple juice does each guest drink?

   _____ gallon

4. Four pasta servings are left over after dinner. They are equal to $\frac{1}{14}$ of the total. How many pasta servings were made?

   _____ servings

5. Each guest drinks about $1\frac{3}{4}$ cups of coffee. This amount is $\frac{2}{3}$ of the amount of coffee provided for each guest. How much coffee is provided for each guest?

   _____ cups

6. The caterer prepares 4 dinners for guests with special diets. This is $\frac{1}{13}$ of the total meals. How many meals does the caterer prepare in total?

   _____ meals

NAME _____

Check What You Know

Customary Measurement

Read the problem carefully and solve. Show your work under each question.

Young Chef Cooking School trains young people to be cooks. The students are taught all kinds of cooking skills. These skills include knowing the common tools and measurements in the kitchen.

1. Tim bakes a large rectangular cake for a party. The cake is 3 feet and 7 inches long. How many inches long is the cake he bakes?

_____43_____ in.

2. Nick makes a recipe that calls for 6 pints of milk. How many cups of milk does he need?

_____12_____ c.

3. In one recipe for bread, Cesar uses 96 ounces of flour. How many pounds of flour does he use?

_____6_____ lb.

4. Donald measures the width of the large oven before he bakes some pizzas. The oven is 2 yards wide. How many inches wide is the oven?

_____72_____ in.

5. Bella cooks 12 quarts of soup. How many gallons of soup does she cook?

_____3_____ gal.

6. Dennis bakes 7 pounds 10 ounces of potatoes one day. How many ounces of potatoes does he bake?

_____122_____ oz.

NAME _____

Check What You Know

Customary Measurement

Read the problem carefully and solve. Show your work under each question.

In the Tyler Middle School science classes, the students learn how to take measurements. Students measure units that change, like temperature and time. They also measure the size of fixed objects in the classroom.

1. Kurt looks at the scale on the thermometer below. What is the temperature?

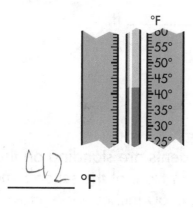

__42__ °F

2. Dale measures the perimeter of the triangle below. What is the perimeter of the triangle?

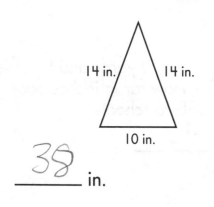

14 in. 14 in. 10 in.

__38__ in.

3. Robert measures the length and the width of the classroom. The rectangular room measures 9 yards by 7 yards. What is the area of the room?

_____ sq. yd.

4. How much time has passed between the two clocks?

__1__ hour __44__ minutes

5. Yolanda measures the volume of a pencil box below. What is its volume?

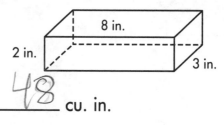

8 in. 2 in. 3 in.

__48__ cu. in.

Lesson 9.1 Units of Length (inches, feet, yards, and miles)

Read the problem carefully and solve. Show your work under each question.

Most students at Morton County School walk to school. The longest distance any student walks is more than a mile. The shortest distance is less than a football field. Most students live within half a mile of the school.

Helpful Hint

These are the values of customary units of length:

1 foot (ft.) = 12 inches (in.)

1 yard (yd.) = 3 feet = 36 inches

1 mile (mi.) = 5,280 feet = 1,760 yards

1. The front door of Douglas's home is 21 feet and 7 inches from the school fence. How many inches is the door from the school fence?

_____ in.

2. Olga lives 26 yards and 2 feet from Douglas's home. How many feet is her home from Douglas's?

_____ ft.

3. Javier lives 1 mile and 12 yards from the school. How many feet does he live from the school?

_____ ft.

4. Some students are standing on the sidewalk in front of the school. The sidewalk is 60 inches wide. How wide is the sidewalk in feet?

_____ ft.

5. Shana walks 70 yards and 4 inches to school. How far in inches does Shana walk to school?

_____ in.

Lesson 9.2 Liquid Volume (cups, pints, quarts, and gallons)

Read the problem carefully and solve. Show your work under each question.

Platter Restaurant serves family-style meals for breakfast, lunch, and dinner. The restaurant is very busy, so the cooks have to make large batches of the recipes.

Helpful Hint

These are customary units of liquid volume:

1 pint (pt.) = 2 cups (c.)
1 quart (qt.) = 2 pints
1 gallon (gal.) = 4 quarts

1. One day, Michael mixes 14 gallons of lemonade. How many quarts is this?

_____ qt.

2. One pudding recipe calls for 7 quarts and 1 pint of milk. How many pints of milk are needed?

_____ pt.

3. Nora uses a juice machine to make 12 pints of lemon juice. How many quarts of lemon juice does she make?

_____ qt.

4. Sarah makes pancake batter. The recipe uses 2 pints and 1 cup of vegetable oil. How many cups of oil are in the batter?

_____ c.

5. A recipe for spaghetti sauce takes 12 quarts and 1 pint of tomato sauce. How many pints of sauce is that?

_____ pt.

Lesson 9.3 Weight (ounces, pounds, and tons)

Read the problem carefully and solve. Show your work under each question.

Candy makers sell their products by the ounce or by the pound. When they make candy, they measure the weight in tens and hundreds of pounds. They often ship their products by the ton.

> **Helpful Hint**
>
> These are customary units of weight:
>
> 1 pound (lb.) = 16 ounces (oz.)
> 2,000 pounds = 1 ton (T.)

1. Tasty Delights are sold in packages that weigh 2 pounds and 6 ounces. How many ounces of candy are in each package?

    _____ oz.

2. Hand-dipped chocolates are sold in boxes that weigh 80 ounces. How many pounds of hand-dipped chocolates are in a box?

    _____ lb.

3. A shipment of boxes of Crackling Surprises weighs 2 tons and 650 pounds. How much does the shipment weigh in pounds?

    _____ lb.

4. A truck carries 24,000 pounds of various hard candies. How many tons of candy does the truck carry?

    _____ T.

5. A box contains 240 ounces of caramel candies in 2-ounce bags. How many pounds of caramel candies are in the box?

    _____ lb.

Lesson 9.4 Temperature

Read the problem carefully and solve. Show your work under each question.

Mr. Shim's science class studies weather patterns. Students keep track of the temperature during the school year. They see how the temperature changes with the seasons. The unit for temperature is degrees.

Helpful Hint

Here are important Fahrenheit temperatures.

212°F = water boils

32°F = water freezes

98.6°F = normal body temperature

1. One day, the temperature drops until it reaches the point that water freezes. Mark the freezing temperature of water on the thermometer below.

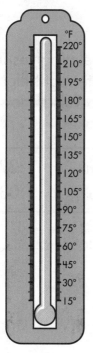

2. Early one morning, Grace records the temperature as 64 degrees Fahrenheit. By noon, the temperature has gone up 15 degrees Fahrenheit. What is the noon temperature?

_____ °F

3. Kevin notices that the temperature is 57 degrees Fahrenheit. Mark the thermometer below to show 57 degrees Fahrenheit.

4. Malcolm records the temperature as 91 degrees Fahrenheit. A storm comes and the temperature drops 23 degrees Fahrenheit. What is the temperature after the storm?

_____ °F

Lesson 9.5 Elapsed Time

Read the problem carefully and solve. Show your work under each question.

Bluejay Airlines has flights from Midland to many cities. Some of the flights are short and others are long. Passengers can choose the time for arrival or departure.

Helpful Hint

Do these steps to find the elapsed time.

1. Count the whole hours between start and end.
2. Count the minutes remaining.
3. Add the hours and minutes.

1. Mr. Desai has to get up early for a flight. He goes to bed at 11:14 p.m. The time he gets up is shown on the clock to the right. How much sleep does he get?

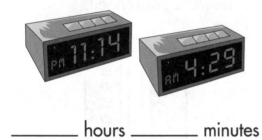

_____ hours _____ minutes

2. A passenger misses the first flight one morning. The ticket agent tells the passenger when the next flight will leave. Both departure times are shown below. How long is the time between flights?

| Departure 1: | 9:15 a.m. |
| Departure 2: | 2:01 p.m. |

_____ hours _____ minutes

3. Ms. Warren expects her daughter to arrive later this afternoon. The left clock shows the time now. The right clock shows the arrival time. How long must Ms. Warren wait for her daughter to arrive?

_____ hours _____ minutes

4. The sign below gives information about a late-night flight from Midland to Tulsa. How long does the flight take?

| Departure: | 11:22 p.m. |
| Arrival: | 1:03 a.m. |

_____ hours _____ minutes

Lesson 9.6 Measuring Perimeter and Area

Read the problem carefully and solve. Show your work under each question.

The Highland Paving Company paves areas ranging from a few square feet to many square yards. The company has special rates for paving small areas. The manager makes a scale drawing for each job so he knows how much material is needed to complete the project.

Helpful Hint

Perimeter is the sum of the sides of a figure.

Area is the number of square units that cover a surface. To find the area of a rectangle or square, multiply the length times the width.

1. A place to park bicycles at a school is in the shape of a triangle. What is the perimeter of the triangle?

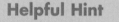

_____ ft.

2. The diagram below shows the area of an old sidewalk that needs to be repaved. What is the area of the sidewalk?

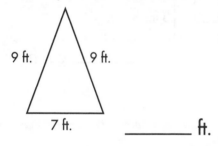

_____ sq. ft.

3. The diagram below is a scale drawing of a paving project. To finish the paving, it needs edging. What is the perimeter of the project?

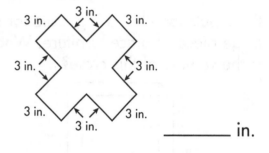

_____ in.

4. The diagram shows a driveway that will be paved. What is the area of the driveway?

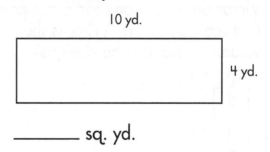

_____ sq. yd.

Lesson 9.7 Measuring Volume

Read the problem carefully and solve. Show your work under each question.

The Pack-It Box Company makes boxes and crates. The boxes range from a few inches on a side to several feet. The crates range from a few feet to a few yards.

> **Helpful Hint**
>
> **Volume** is the number of cubic (cu.) units that fill a solid object. To find the volume of a solid with rectangular sides, multiply the length, width, and height together.

3. Pack-It's watch box is a cube. What is the volume of the box?

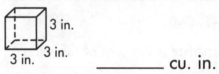

_____ cu. in.

1. Boris puts together a big crate for a large piece of office furniture. What is the volume of this crate?

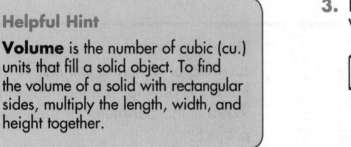

4. Pam prepares boxes for a toy company. What is the volume of each box?

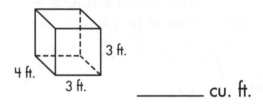

_____ cu. ft.

2. Victor designs a box for a company that makes mirrors. What is the volume of the box he designs?

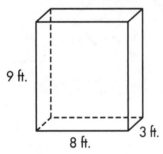

_____ cu. ft.

5. Karen builds a crate to ship a huge machine. What is the volume of the crate?

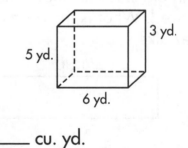

_____ cu. yd.

Lesson 9.8 Measuring Volume

Read the problem carefully and solve. Show your work under each question.

Sally is finding the volume of different objects on her math test. She broke apart the following object into parts, and then found the volume.

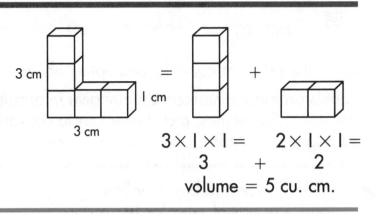

$$3 \times 1 \times 1 = 3$$ $$2 \times 1 \times 1 = 2$$
$$3 \quad + \quad 2$$
volume = 5 cu. cm.

Helpful Hint

To find the **volume** of irregular objects, first break them into parts. Then, find the volume of each part (multiply length, width, and height). Finally, add the volume of the parts together.

1. Draw how you would decompose this object.

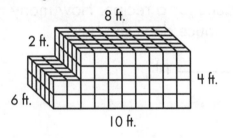

2. Find the volume of this object.

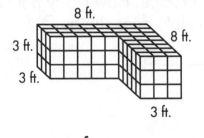

_____ cu. ft.

3. What is the volume of this object?

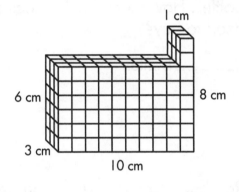

_____ cu. cm.

4. Find the volume of this object.

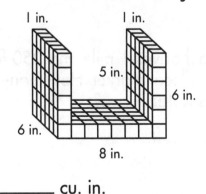

_____ cu. in.

Check What You Learned

Customary Measurement

CHAPTER 9 POSTTEST

Read the problem carefully and solve. Show your work under each question.

Labels on food containers usually give information about the weight or volume of the items. Sometimes, a customer has to convert from one set of units to another. Changing units can make shopping easier.

1. Wendy wants to buy 1 gallon and 3 quarts of juice for her party guests. The juice is sold in 1-quart bottles. How many bottles does she need to buy?

   _____ bottles

2. Ron buys 7 pounds and 2 ounces of apples. How many ounces of apples does he buy?

   _____ oz.

3. Rafael drives 1 mile and 250 feet to the local market. How many feet does Rafael drive?

   _____ ft.

4. The foil package that Dani buys in the store contains 55 yards of foil. How many feet of foil is this?

   _____ ft.

5. Rita gets 2 quarts and 1 pint of sauce for a recipe. How many pints of sauce does she buy?

   _____ pt.

6. Eliza buys 64 ounces of chocolate for a recipe. How many pounds of chocolate does she buy?

   _____ lb.

Check What You Learned

Customary Measurement

Read the problem carefully and solve. Show your work under each question.

The Pleasant Living Home Store sells many products that make homes more enjoyable. Some products are ready to use. Other products, like paint, have to be applied or installed in the home.

---

1. Deanne buys a digital clock. She checks the time in the morning and in the afternoon. The times are shown below. How much time has passed?

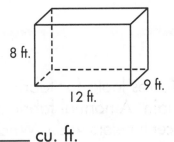

_____ hours _____ minutes

2. Rochelle measures the volume of a room to decide how much air freshener to use. What is its volume?

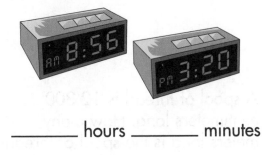

8 ft.   12 ft.   9 ft.

_____ cu. ft.

3. Charlie wants to repaint one wall in a room. The wall measures 9 feet tall by 14 feet long. What is the area of the wall?

_____ sq. ft.

4. Walt reads the outdoor thermometer. What is the outside temperature?

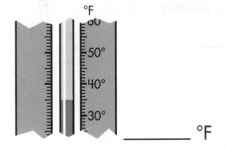

°F

50°

40°

30°

_____ °F

5. Helen measures the size of a room to see if a certain rug will fit in the room. What is the perimeter and area of the room?

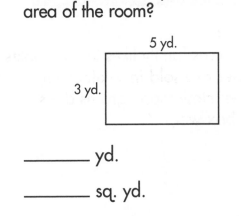

5 yd.

3 yd.

_____ yd.

_____ sq. yd.

Check What You Know

Metric Measurement

Read the problem carefully and solve. Show your work under each question.

Ms. Torres travels in Europe and is familiar with metric units. Today, she shops with her children, Pete and Sonia, for groceries and for fabrics.

1. At the grocery store, Pete asks for some soda in 2-liter bottles. Ms. Torres buys 8 bottles. How many milliliters does she get?

_____ mL

4. The store sells olive oil in bottles that hold 750 milliliters. How many liters of olive oil do 20 of these bottles hold?

_____ L

2. Sonia likes packaged dinners. Small dinners have 300 grams of food. If they buy 10 dinners, how many kilograms of food is this?

_____ kg

5. A spool of thread is 12,300 centimeters long. How many meters long is the spool of thread?

_____ m

3. The Torres family likes to eat apples. Apples are sold in 9-kilogram boxes. How many grams does one box weigh?

_____ g

6. Ms. Torres looks for fabric to make a curtain. A normal fabric roll is 114 centimeters wide. What is this width in millimeters?

_____ mm

Check What You Know

Metric Measurement

Read the problem carefully and solve. Show your work under each question.

Weather balloons are sent up into the sky from weather stations. As the balloons float up, they send back radio signals. Weather balloons measure the temperature, wind speed, and air pressure. Those measurements are used to predict the weather.

1. Balloon 1 is sent up from a weather station. The thermometer shows the temperature at the ground. What is the temperature?

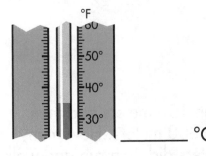

_____ °C

2. Balloon 1 is launched from a shed like the one in the diagram. The base of the shed is a square. What is the perimeter and area of the base?

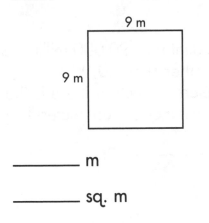

_____ m

_____ sq. m

3. The radio for the balloon has the dimensions shown in the diagram. What is the volume of the radio?

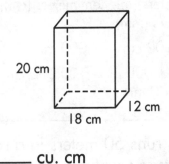

_____ cu. cm

4. A weather forecaster draws a rectangle on a map where the balloon might go. The rectangle on the map is 4 centimeters by 7 centimeters. What is the area on the map?

_____ sq. cm

5. The balloon lands somewhere in a square area that measures 12 kilometers on each side. How large is the area?

_____ sq. km

Lesson 10.1 Units of Length (millimeters, centimeters, meters, and kilometers

Read the problem carefully and solve. Show your work under each question.

Cortez Middle School has a 400-meter track for sports. In physical education classes, students run races of 50 meters, 100 meters, and 200 meters. Sometimes, the teacher has students walk 400 meters or 800 meters.

Helpful Hint

Metric units of length include kilometers (km), meters (m), centimeters (cm), and millimeters (mm).

1 m = 100 cm = 1,000 mm

1 km = 1,000 m = 100,000 cm = 1,000,000 mm

3. Aretha walks 65,000 centimeters. How many meters does she walk?

_____ m

1. Curtis runs 50 meters in a race. How many centimeters does he run?

_____ cm

4. Beth ran 100 meters and then walked 800 meters. How many millimeters did Beth run and walk in total?

_____ mm

2. Leon wears gym shoes that are 22 centimeters long. How many millimeters long are Leon's shoes?

_____ mm

5. One student runs 90,000 millimeters, and another runs 20,000 centimeters. Which of these is the longer distance in centimeters?

_____ cm

Lesson 10.2 Liquid Volume (milliliters, liters, and kiloliters)

Read the problem carefully and solve. Show your work under each question.

The Beverage Mart sells a large amount of sodas, sparkling juices, and bottled water. The containers are marked in metric units.

Helpful Hint

Metric units of liquid volume include these:

1 liter (L) = 1,000 milliliters (mL)
1 kiloliter (kL) = 1,000 liters (L)
1 kiloliter (kL) = 1,000,000 milliliters (mL)

1. Mr. Winslow sells 12 liters of soda to a customer for a birthday party. How many milliliters of soda does the customer buy?

_____ mL

2. Some soft drinks are sold in cans that contain 400 milliliters. How many liters of soda would 10 of these cans contain in total?

_____ L

3. The store sells 3 kiloliters of one popular soft drink every month. How many liters of this soft drink does the store sell every month?

_____ L

4. One day, the store sells 50,000 milliliters of sparkling juice and 60 liters of bottled water. Which is the greater volume?

_____

5. The store sells water bottles that each contain 500 milliliters of water. If the store sells a total of 25,000 milliliters of water, how many bottles are sold?

_____ bottles

Lesson 10.3 Weight (milligrams, grams, and kilograms)

Read the problem carefully and solve. Show your work under each question.

At the Neighborhood Grocery Store, some foods are sold by weight. The weights are measured in metric units.

Helpful Hint

These are metric units of weight:

1 gram (g) = 1,000 milligrams (mg)
1 kilogram (kg) = 1,000 grams
1 kilogram = 1,000,000 milligrams

1. The grocery store sells potatoes in bags that weigh 5 kilograms. How many milligrams do 10 bags of potatoes hold?

_____ mg

2. Quick-cooking rice is sold in boxes that weigh 500 grams each. If the store sells 140 of these boxes, how many kilograms of rice are sold?

_____ kg

3. Mr. Tanaka buys a bag of flour that weighs 2 kilograms. How many grams does the bag of flour weigh?

_____ g

4. Monique buys a bag of apples that weighs 4,000,000 milligrams. What is the weight of the bag of apples in kilograms?

_____ kg

5. Will buys lettuce that sells for $3 per kilogram. He spends $9 on lettuce. How many grams of lettuce does he buy?

_____ g

Lesson 10.4 Temperature

Read the problem carefully and solve. Show your work under each question.

Mr. Shim's science class studies weather patterns. Students record the temperature during the days of the school year. The class uses thermometers marked in degrees Celsius.

Helpful Hint

Here are important Celsius temperatures.

0°C = water freezes

37°C = normal body temperature

100°C = water boils

1. Early one morning, the outside temperature is 2°C. Later that day, the temperature increases by 9°C. What is the temperature then?

_____°C

2. The partial thermometer below shows the zone of human body temperature. Mark the thermometer to show the temperature of 36°C.

3. George boils water in a pan and then checks the temperature of the water. Mark the boiling temperature of water on the thermometer below.

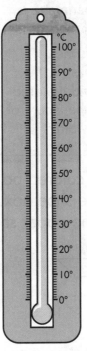

4. Tamara cools a mixture of water and salt. She checks the temperature after 5 minutes. It is 14°C. Mark the thermometer to show the temperature of 14°C.

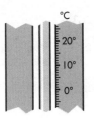

Lesson 10.5 Measuring Perimeter and Area

Read the problem carefully and solve. Show your work under each question.

In Ms. Simon's art class, students decorate shoe boxes. The project encourages students to be creative and think of new ideas. Each shoe box measures 18 cm wide, 12 cm tall, and 28 cm long.

> **Helpful Hint**
>
> The **perimeter** is the distance around an object. The perimeter is the sum of the lengths of the sides.
>
> The **area** of an object is the number of **square units** (sq.) needed to cover it. To find the area of a rectangle, multiply the length of the rectangle times the width.

3. Tom cuts small triangles to use as box decorations. What is the perimeter of each triangle in millimeters?

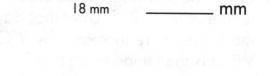

_____ mm

1. Kathy cuts a piece of colored paper to go on the top of the shoe box. What is the area of the paper she cuts?

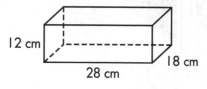

_____ sq. cm

4. Ms. Simon has a roll of wrapping paper. A piece 60 centimeters long is used to wrap one box. How many meters of wrapping paper are needed to wrap 100 boxes?

_____ m

2. Linnell wants to put a ribbon around the top of the box. What is the perimeter of the top?

_____ cm

5. Patrick makes rectangles for decorations. The rectangles measure 2 centimeters by 3 centimeters. What is the total area of 50 rectangles?

_____ sq. cm

Lesson 10.6 Measuring Volume

Read the problem carefully and solve. Show your work under each question.

Quiet Air Company supplies heating and air-conditioning services. The company measures the volume of each room to supply the correct amount of heat and cool air throughout a building. Quiet Air measures the size of each room using the metric system.

Helpful Hint

To find the **volume** of a space with sides shaped like rectangles, multiply the measure of the length, the width, and the height.

Cubic units (cu.) are used for volumes.

1. The diagram below shows the measurements of a room the company will heat. What is the volume of the room?

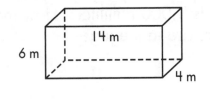

_____ cu. m

2. The diagram below shows the dimensions of a space for an air conditioner. What is the volume of this space?

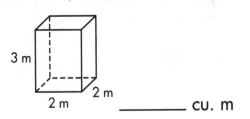

_____ cu. m

3. The diagram below shows the measurements of the entrance to an office building. What is the volume of the entrance?

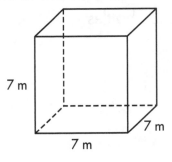

_____ cu. m

4. A wall thermostat controls the temperature in a room. The thermostat has the dimensions shown in the diagram below. What is the volume of the thermostat?

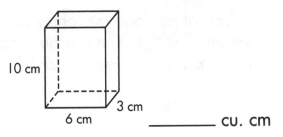

_____ cu. cm

Check What You Learned

Metric Measurement

Read the problem carefully and solve. Show your work under each question.

After their shopping trip, the Torres family examines the items they bought. They check the labels and the quantities of their purchases. They use metric units to measure the items.

1. Pete picks up a bottle of steak sauce that holds 250 milliliters. How many bottles would equal 2 liters?

   _____ bottles

2. Sonia stretches out a piece of fabric that is 4 meters long. How long is the fabric in millimeters?

   _____ mm

3. A bag of pet food the family bought weighs 5,000,000 milligrams. How many kilograms does it weigh?

   _____ kg

4. During the shopping trip, the family drove 7 kilometers. How many centimeters did they go?

   _____ cm

5. Pete puts away a jug of juice that holds 4,000 milliliters. How many liters are in the jug?

   _____ L

6. Some potatoes in the bag weigh 270 grams. How many milligrams do these potatoes weigh?

   _____ mg

Check What You Learned

Metric Measurement

Read the problem carefully and solve. Show your work under each question.

The Cougars football team plays a game in cold, rainy weather. Before the game, the field crew has to put new chalk lines around the edge of the field. The field crew has some other work to do before the game.

1. Two hours before the game, the coach looks at the thermometer. What is the temperature?

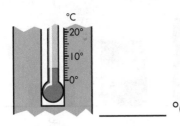

_____ °C

2. The diagram shows the size of the Cougars football field in meters. What is the perimeter of the field?

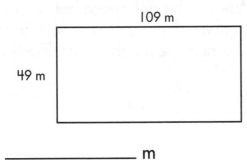

_____ m

3. What is the area of the Cougars football field in square meters?

_____ sq. m

4. The field crew stores their tools and machines in a room under the stadium. The diagram shows the shape and dimensions of the room. What is the volume of the room?

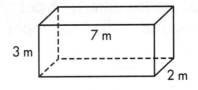

_____ cu. m

5. The field crew sets up a tent with a rectangular roof. The roof measures 5 meters by 3 meters. What is the area of the roof in square centimeters?

_____ sq. cm

Check What You Know

Graphs and Probability

Read the problem carefully and solve. Show your work under each question.

Music tastes of students are different in different areas of the country. Music tastes also change from year to year. A survey of the students at Metro School gave the results shown in the graph to the right. Use the graph to answer the questions.

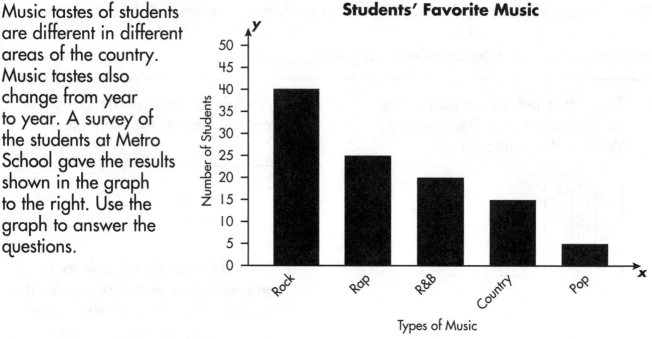

Students' Favorite Music

Types of Music

1. What are the different types of music represented in the bar graph?

   _____

   _____

2. How many students like Rap music best?

   _____ students

3. How many students like Pop music best?

   _____ students

4. How many students in total like Rock and Country music?

   _____ students

5. What is the difference between the number of students who like Rock best and the number who like Rap best?

   _____ students

6. How many students were surveyed in all?

   _____

Check What You Know

Graphs and Probability

Read the problem carefully and solve. Show your work under each question.

Taste Good Bakery bakes bread by the truckload. The bakery ships the bread to stores up to 100 miles away. The amount of bread baked in the last seven days is 33, 20, 35, 40, 26, 20, and 15 truckloads.

1. What is the range of the data?

_____

4. What is the median of the data?

_____

2. What is the mode of the data?

_____

5. What was the chance that on any day the number of truckloads of bread baked was 40?

_____

3. What is the mean of the data?

_____

6. What was the chance that on any day the number of truckloads of bread baked was 20?

_____

Lesson 11.1 Bar Graphs

Read the problem carefully and solve. Show your work under each question.

Mr. Garcia's class collects bottles to be recycled. They record the number of bottles collected each day for one week. They collect 25 bottles on Monday, 20 on Tuesday, and 40 on Wednesday. On Thursday, they collect 25 bottles, and on Friday they collect 15 bottles. The class plans to make a graph of this data.

Helpful Hint

1. The **x axis** represents the day of the week.

2. The **y axis** represents the number of bottles collected.

1. Use the information above to draw a bar graph for Mr. Garcia's class. Include labels for the x axis and the y axis. Add a title.

2. How many more bottles were collected on Monday than Friday?

_____ bottles

3. On which days did the students collect the same number of bottles?

_____

4. How many total bottles did the class collect in the week?

_____ bottles

5. Between which two days in a row did the number of bottles collected change the most?

_____

Lesson 11.2 Line Graphs

Read the problem carefully and solve. Show your work under each question.

The Dragons football team keeps a record of the number of points the team scores each game. For the eight games of the season, the team scored these points: (Game 1) 18, (Game 2) 34, (Game 3) 28, (Game 4) 14, (Game 5) 25, (Game 6) 7, (Game 7) 17, (Game 8) 20.

Helpful Hint

The *x* axis represents each game of the season. The *y* axis represents the points scored.

1. Use the information above to draw a line graph for the Dragons football team. Include labels for the *x* axis and the *y* axis. Add a title.

2. In which game did the team score the most points?

   Game _____

3. In which game did the team score the fewest points?

   Game _____

4. Between which two games did the number of points scored increase the most?

   Game _____ and

   Game _____

5. Between which two games did the number of points scored decrease the most?

   Game _____ and

   Game _____

Lesson 11.3 Calculating the Mean

Read the problem carefully and solve. Show your work under each question.

Mr. Barnett's math class collects some numerical data to use in class. Each group of numerical data they collect is recorded. The students then calculate the mean for each group of data.

> **Helpful Hint**
>
> The average of a set of numbers is the **mean**. A **data set** is a set of numbers.
>
> To find the mean, add all the numbers in a set and divide by the number of values in the set.

1. Six students report the hours of homework they each do throughout the week. The hours recorded by the students are 2, 5, 3, 4, 6, and 4. What is the mean number of hours for this data?

   _____ hours

2. Ethan counts the number of water bottles sold in the lunchroom. For five days, the bottles sold are 24, 35, 47, 41, and 38. How many bottles on average are sold each day?

   _____ bottles

3. Seven students count how many songs they each hear in one day. The students create the following data set with this information: 9, 22, 15, 19, 12, 27, and 29. What is the mean for the number of songs heard in one day?

   _____ songs

4. Megan counts the number of cars in a school parking lot after school for eight days. She counts 23, 15, 11, 24, 19, 34, 27, and 7 cars parked over the eight days. What is the mean value for the number of cars parked in the lot after school?

   _____ cars

Lesson 11.4 Calculating the Median, Mode, and Range

Read the problem carefully and solve. Show your work under each question.

The Athletics Booster Club helps support school sports by selling snacks and drinks at games during the year. Students and parents work together at the snack shack during the games.

Helpful Hint

The **median** is the value that is in the middle of a set of data when the data is put in order from least to greatest.

The **mode** is the value that occurs most often in a data set.

The **range** is the difference between the value of the largest number in the data set and the smallest number in the data set.

1. In six games, the snack shack sold different numbers of cups of hot chocolate. The numbers of cups of hot chocolate sold were 22, 13, 35, 19, 29, and 37. What is the range of this data?

_____ cups

2. Mr. Washington counts the number of nickels customers use to pay for snacks at seven games. He counts 27, 14, 22, 15, 19, 11, and 23 nickels for the seven games. What is the median of this data?

_____ nickels

3. Bottled water is a popular drink when the weather is warm. During the spring, the snack shack sold 44, 37, 53, 49, 51, 37, and 52 bottles of water at seven games. What is the mode of this set?

_____ bottles

Lesson 11.5 Calculating Probability

Read the problem carefully and solve. Show your work under each question.

Ms. Pearl has reward bags for students in her kindergarten class. When a student does well, Ms. Pearl lets the student draw a reward slip from one of the bags. The student uses the slip to claim the actual reward.

Helpful Hint

Probability is the chance that an event will occur. An **outcome** is whether an event occurs or not.

To calculate the probability, divide the number of outcomes desired by the total number of possible outcomes.

1. One reward bag contains 10 slips for pandas, 6 slips for monkeys, 6 slips for lions, and 8 slips for kittens. What is the chance of drawing a slip for a panda?

   _____

2. There is a reward bag for toys that has 15 slips for cars, 8 slips for trucks, 7 slips for airplanes, and 5 slips for boats. What is the chance of getting a reward slip for a boat?

   _____

3. One reward bag contains 10 slips for erasers, 20 slips for pencils, 5 slips for pens, and 5 slips for scissors. What is the chance of drawing slip for a pencil?

   _____

4. One bag contains 14 slips for combs, 2 slips for small brushes, 8 slips for hair clips, and 4 slips for small mirrors. What is the chance of getting a slip for a small brush?

   _____

5. The last reward bag contains 11 slips for crackers, 16 slips for apples, 13 slips for dried fruit, and 10 slips for peanuts. What is the chance of drawing a slip for peanuts?

   _____

Check What You Learned

Graphs and Probability

Read the problem carefully and solve. Show your work under each question.

Schools keep records of student absences throughout the school year. The cumulative absences from Lakeland School for one semester are displayed in the graph to the right. Use the graph to answer the questions.

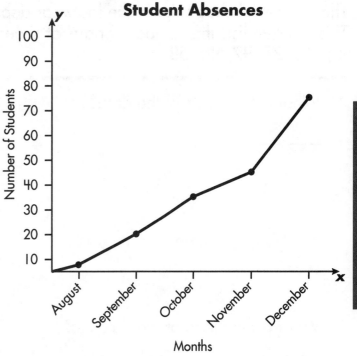

Student Absences

Months

1. In which month was the greatest number of students absent?

   _____

2. How many students were absent in September?

   _____ students

3. How many students were absent in November?

   _____ students

4. What is the difference between the number of students absent in August and the number of students absent in December?

   _____ students

5. In which month were 35 students absent?

   _____

6. How many more students were absent in November and December than were absent in August and September?

   _____ students

Check What You Learned

Graphs and Probability

Read the problem carefully and solve. Show your work under each question.

The number of shoe sales in the footwear department varies from week to week. This data set lists the number of pairs of shoes sold each week in the last 7 weeks: 42, 35, 27, 47, 44, 58, and 27.

1. What is the mode of the data?

_____

2. What is the mean of the data set?

_____

3. What is the range of the data set?

_____

4. What is the median of this data set?

_____

5. What was the chance that in any week the number of pairs of shoes sold was 27?

_____

6. What was the chance that in any week the number of pairs of shoes sold was 42?

_____

Check What You Know

Geometry

Read the problem carefully and solve. Show your work under each question.

Park planners make plans for small and large parks. Often, the final plans are quite complex. However, even complex plans are made of simple parts. Students at Marshall School look carefully at some park plans to find the simpler parts.

1. Joanne looks at this diagram. Does the diagram show a line or a line segment? What is the name of the figure?

S — T

_____

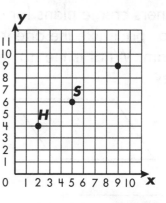

2. Sheila finds the lines below in the plans. Is this pair of lines parallel, perpendicular, or intersecting?

_____

3. Ross sees the image below in the park plans. Use the labels to name what he sees.

K
  L

_____

4. A location on the park plan is labeled point S. What ordered pair represents point S?

_____

5. Another location is labeled point H. What ordered pair represents point H?

_____

6. A cemetery is located at ordered pair (9, 9). Label this point C.

Check What You Know

Geometry

Read the problem carefully and solve. Show your work under each question.

Landscape designers draw artistic plans for gardens. The plans are drawn to scale so that people who install the landscapes can order what is needed. Designers often work with unusual shapes.

1. Designers create plans for a garden to fit a space like the one in the diagram. What is the name of this shape?

   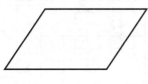

   _____

2. Stepping stones in the Kwon garden are placed to look like the shape below. What is the name of this shape?

   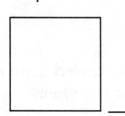

   _____

3. The Patterson family wants a fountain that is shaped like the figure below. Describe the surfaces of the figure.

   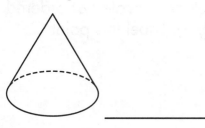

   _____

4. Below is a plan for a section of patio at the Flores home. What is the name of this shape?

   _____

5. The Antonelli family builds a garden that has the shape shown below. What is the name of this shape?

   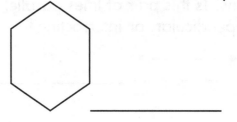

   _____

6. Ms. Gibson plans a simple flower bed for a client. The shape of the flower bed is shown below. What is the name of this shape?

   _____

Lesson 12.1 Points, Lines, Rays, and Angles

Read the problem carefully and solve. Show your work under each question.

Mr. Spencer's math class studies the use of symbols in math. Right now, the students are studying symbols used in geometry. Mr. Spencer shows examples of how the symbols are used. He asks the students to draw diagrams that are like his examples.

Helpful Hint

The symbol for a **point** is a dot.

A **line** passes through two points.

An **angle** is made of two **rays** starting from the same point.

The point where the two rays connect is called the **vertex**.

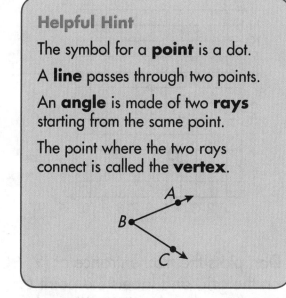

1. Helga draws line segment $\overline{AB}$. Draw and label a line segment $\overline{CD}$ in the space below.

A _____ B

2. Ellis describes ray $\overrightarrow{AB}$ shown below. He says the ray starts at point A, passes through B, and extends forever. Draw and label a ray $\overrightarrow{EF}$ in the space below.

A _____ B

3. Terry sees that line $\overleftrightarrow{AB}$ passes through points A and B. This line is shown below. In the space below, draw and label the line $\overleftrightarrow{KL}$.

4. Ariel draws an angle shown below on the board. She labels the angle. Name the rays, the vertex, and the angle.

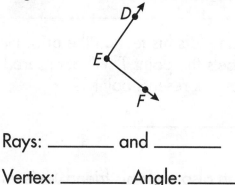

Rays: _____ and _____

Vertex: _____ Angle: _____

5. Joan draws the angle shown below on her paper. Name the angle, rays, and the vertex.

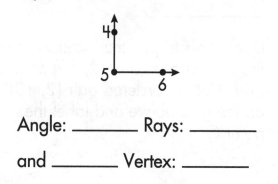

Angle: _____ Rays: _____

and _____ Vertex: _____

Lesson 12.2 Ordered Pairs on a Coordinate Plane

Read the problem carefully and solve. Show your work under each question.

Dan decides to show the location of some places at his campsite using a grid. He locates these places by plotting and labeling the points on a grid.

Helpful Hint

On a grid, the *x* axis runs on a horizontal line. The *y* axis runs on a vertical line.

A point on a grid is located by using an ordered pair. An ordered pair lists a point on the *x* axis first, then one on the *y* axis: (5, 3).

Points located on the same grid are called **coordinate points** or **coordinates**.

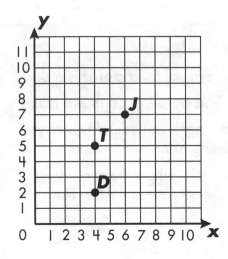

1. Dan plots his tent on the grid. He labels the point *T*. What ordered pair represents point *T*?

   _____

2. Dan also plots his friend Joe's tent on the grid. He labels the point *J*. What ordered pair represents point *J*?

   _____

3. Dan wants to plot the location of the campfire area at (2, 10) on the grid. Plot the ordered pair (2, 10) on the grid above and label the point *C*.

4. Dan plots the trail entrance at (9, 4) on the grid and labels the point *E*. Plot the ordered pair (9, 4) on the grid and label the point *E*.

5. The dog park is labeled with the point *D*. What ordered pair represents this location?

   _____

6. The boat rental at the lake is located at ordered pair (9, 11). Plot this point and label it *B*.

Lesson 12.3 Parallel and Perpendicular Lines

Read the problem carefully and solve. Show your work under each question.

Ms. Tsai's social studies class studies geography. Students study how mapmakers create maps. Students draw street maps of their neighborhoods as an assignment.

Helpful Hint

Parallel lines never intersect.

Intersecting lines touch at exactly one point.

Perpendicular lines touch at exactly one point and form right angles.

1. Norm draws a section of a street that looks like the lines shown in the diagram. What are these lines called?

_____ lines

2. Mia draws a diagram of two streets that cross like the lines shown below. What kind of lines are these?

_____ lines

3. Janet knows that the sides of her street are parallel. She labels two points on one side of the street *J* and *L*. She labels two points on the other side of the street *F* and *H*. Draw two parallel lines with these labels.

4. Vicky draws a street corner that looks like the diagram below. What kind of lines are these?

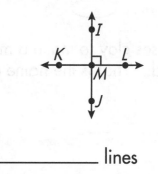

_____ lines

5. Stan draws two lines that intersect but do not form right angles. The lines are $\overleftrightarrow{ST}$ and $\overleftrightarrow{UV}$. They cross at point *R*. Draw and label a diagram of the two lines.

Lesson 12.4 Solid Figures

Read the problem carefully and solve. Show your work under each question.

Two of Mr. Solomon's fifth-grade math classes build models of solid figures. Students will get rewards for skillful work and good ideas. The students can make the models out of any materials they want to use.

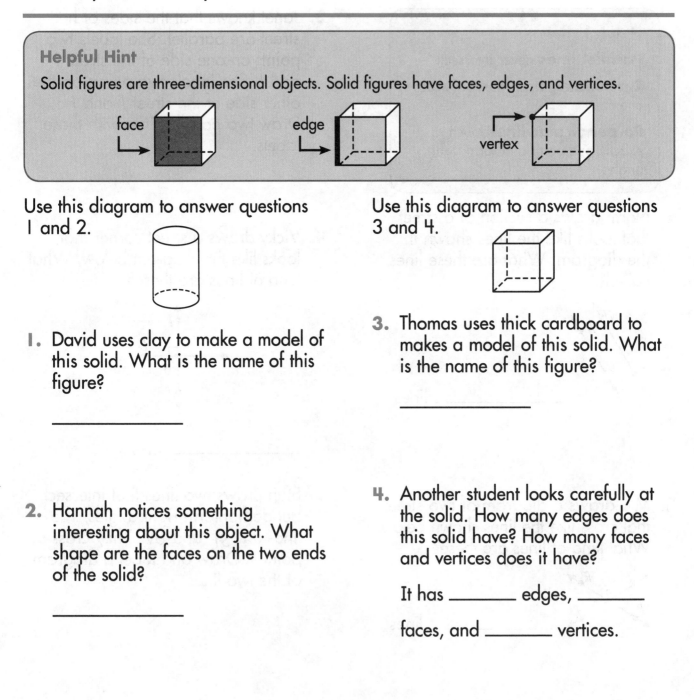

Helpful Hint

Solid figures are three-dimensional objects. Solid figures have faces, edges, and vertices.

face →   edge →   → vertex

Use this diagram to answer questions 1 and 2.

Use this diagram to answer questions 3 and 4.

1. David uses clay to make a model of this solid. What is the name of this figure?

   _____

3. Thomas uses thick cardboard to makes a model of this solid. What is the name of this figure?

   _____

2. Hannah notices something interesting about this object. What shape are the faces on the two ends of the solid?

   _____

4. Another student looks carefully at the solid. How many edges does this solid have? How many faces and vertices does it have?

   It has _____ edges, _____

   faces, and _____ vertices.

Check What You Learned

Geometry

Read the problem carefully and solve. Show your work under each question.

Kits for model boats have detailed directions. The directions have diagrams and written steps. The more complex models have more complex directions. Model boats have many lines and angles.

1. On the directions, Jordan looks at lines that look like the lines below. These lines appear to be what type of lines?

_____

2. On the front of the ship Bessie is building, there is an angle like the one in the diagram below. Name the angle using the labels. What kind of angle is this?

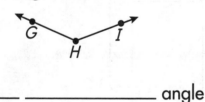

_____ _____ angle

3. Part of a mast looks like the diagram below. Name the figure using the labels.

•C

•D _____

4. Ken measures the angle that the mast makes with the deck of a sailboat. Use a protractor and measure the angle below.

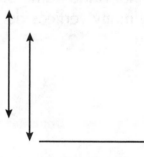 _____

5. The masts of a sailboat are lines like the two shown below. What are these lines called?

_____

6. The corner of a sail has an angle like the one below. Name the angle. What type of angle is it?

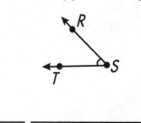

_____ _____ angle

Check What You Learned

Geometry

Read the problem carefully and solve. Show your work under each question.

Interior decorators use many different objects to make homes look more beautiful. Some of these objects have the shapes of flat geometric figures. Others have the shapes of solids.

1. Ms. Holmes decorates a child's bedroom with a set of colorful panels like the one shown below. What is the shape of these panels?

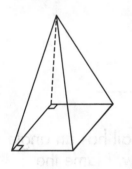

_____

2. Mr. Porter found a clock for a customer. The clock looks like the solid below. What is the name of this solid? How many vertices does it have?

_____

_____ vertices

3. The shape of a tile that is used for decoration in the Tai home is shown below. What is the name of the shape?

_____

4. Mr. Larson uses a large cabinet. The shape of the cabinet is shown below. What is the name of this shape? How many faces does it have? How many edges does it have?

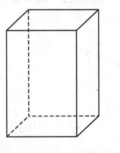

_____

_____ faces

_____ edges

Check What You Know

Preparing for Algebra

Read the problem carefully and solve. Show your work under each question.

An automobile parts store has a huge number of items to repair cars. The manager likes math. Sometimes, he tests his employees to see if they understand math ideas.

1. The serial numbers on a group of batteries end with a 2-digit pattern. The numbers of the batteries in the store are 22, 33, 44, and 55. If the pattern continues, what are the next 2 numbers in the pattern?

   _____, _____

2. A buyer from a repair shop buys a big box of headlights plus 2 individual headlights. If you wrote an expression to represent the total number of batteries purchased, what would the variable represent?

   _____

   _____

3. Manuel uses an equation to find the number of spare tires in the store. The equation is $t - 12 = 25$. Write the equation as an open sentence.

   _____

4. A clerk fills one shelf with cans of oil and has 8 cans left over. If an expression was used to find the total number of cans, what value would the variable represent? Write the situation as a variable expression.

   _____

   _____

5. The part numbers on different types of wiper blades have 3 digits at the end. The numbers form the pattern 358, 361, and 364. What are the next 3 numbers in this pattern?

   _____, _____, _____

Lesson 13.1 Number Patterns

Read the problem carefully and solve. Show your work under each question.

The fifth-grade math class at Shady Valley School looks for number patterns in everyday life. The students find patterns and try to determine the missing numbers in the patterns.

Helpful Hint

Look at the relationship between each pair of successive numbers in a set to find the pattern of the numbers. To find the relationship, subtract one number from the next in the pattern.

1. Martin looks at code numbers on some soup cans. The last four digits on the first can are 7831. On the second can, they are 7835. On the third can, they are 7839. What is the next number in the pattern?

    _____

2. The last two numbers in four school locker combinations are 11, 14, 18, and 23. These numbers make a pattern. What are the next four numbers in this pattern?

    _____

3. Lionel sees that three cars in the school parking lot have these digits in their license plate numbers: 84, 78, and 72. These numbers form a pattern. What are the next three numbers in the pattern?

    _____

4. Shelley looks at the numbers in the prices of three sale items. The numbers are $43, $36, and $29. These numbers make a pattern. What are the next three numbers in the pattern?

    _____

5. Arnold notices some locker numbers that are in a pattern. The locker numbers are 2, 4, 6, 10, and 16. In this pattern, what are the next three numbers?

    _____

Lesson 13.2 Number Sentences

Read the problem carefully and solve. Show your work under each question.

Jack and Tammy play a missing number game. Jack writes a number sentence that has parentheses on both sides of the equal sign. He leaves one number missing from the number sentence. Tammy has to solve his number sentence and find the missing number. Then, Tammy writes a number sentence for Jack to solve.

Helpful Hint

Remember that both sides of a number sentence have to stay equal.

If a number sentence has parentheses in it, perform the operation inside the parentheses first.

1. Jack writes the number sentence below. Find the missing number in Jack's number sentence.

$(13 + 5) + 11 = (11 + 5) + \boxed{}$

2. Tammy writes the number sentence below for Jack to solve. Find the missing number in Tammy's number sentence.

$(12 \times 3) \times 10 = (12 \times 10) \times \boxed{}$

3. Jack writes another number sentence for Tammy to solve. Find the missing number in Jack's number sentence.

$(125 + \boxed{} + 108 = (35 + 108) + 125$

4. Tammy writes another number sentence for Jack to solve. Find the missing number in Tammy's number sentence.

$(23 \times 6) \times \boxed{} = (6 \times 17) \times 23$

Lesson 13.3 Graphing Number Patterns

Read the problem carefully and solve. Show your work under each question.

The table shows the number of miles that Greg and Marcia ran. This can also be shown on a coordinate plane.

Days	Greg's miles	Marcia's miles
0	0	0
1	2	4
2	4	8
3	6	12
4	8	16
5	10	20

1. The ordered pairs for each point for Greg are: (0, 0), (1, 2), (2, 4), (3, 6), (4, 8), and (5, 10). What are the ordered pairs for each point for Marcia?

_____

_____

2. The points for Greg's miles have been plotted on a coordinate plane. Plot the points for Marcia's miles.

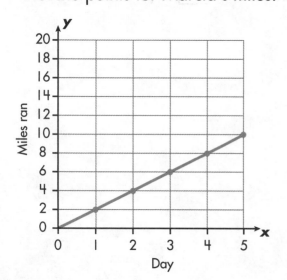

3. Does Greg or Marcia run more miles?

_____

4. Describe the pattern of miles ran.

_____

_____

_____

_____

Lesson 13.4 Variable Expressions

Read the problem carefully and solve. Show your work under each question.

At the local grocery store, the clerks learn to state amounts using variable quantities. They practice saying how much of an item that a shopper buys. The clerks use variable expressions.

Helpful Hint

A **variable** is an unknown quantity. It represents any one of a set of numbers or other objects.

A **variable expression** is a verbal statement. It includes a numerical value and an unknown quantity.

Suppose you have a carton of apples plus 10 apples. The variable represents the number of apples in the carton. The variable expression for the total number of apples is $x + 10$.

1. Keith says a shopper bought a bag of potatoes and 5 additional potatoes. Write words that explain the variable in the situation. Then, write the expression with the variable to show how many potatoes the shopper bought.

   Variable: _____

   _____

   Expression: _____

2. According to Gary, one shopper bought 6 muffins plus a tray of muffins. What does the variable represents in this statement? Also write the expression to show how many muffins were bought.

   Variable: _____

   _____

   Expression: _____

3. Greg sold a case of soup cans that was missing 2 cans to a shopper. Write what the variable represents. Write a variable expression for how many soup cans were sold.

   Variable: _____

   _____

   Expression: _____

4. Lucy sold a bunch of bananas and 8 loose bananas. Write what the variable represents in this statement. Write an expression that shows how many bananas b were sold.

   Variable: _____

   _____

   Expression: _____

Lesson 13.5 Open Sentences

Read the problem carefully and solve. Show your work under each question.

A discount store has a sale on many items. It is a good time for shoppers to get bargains. Shoppers decide how many of each item to buy.

Helpful Hint

An **open sentence** is a math sentence that has a variable (x).

Example: Six times x equals 12.

A sentence with an equals sign is an equation.

Example: $6x = 12$

---

1. Suzie sees that oranges are on sale. She has 11 oranges, but she needs a total of 24 oranges. Write an open sentence that describes this situation. Then, write an equation for the sentence.

   Open sentence: _____

   _____

   Equation: _____

2. Children's socks are on sale. Ms. Ephraim has 9 pairs and wants a total of 12 pairs. Write an open sentence for the pairs of socks p. Then, write an equation for the sentence.

   Open sentence: _____

   _____

   Equation: _____

3. Mark returns 3 T-shirts and is left with 6 T-shirts in all. Write an open sentence for the T-shirts t. Write an equation for the sentence.

   Open sentence: _____

   _____

   Equation: _____

4. Mr. Liu wants 4 times as many golf balls as he now has. He wants 24 golf balls total. Write an open sentence and then write an equation.

   Open sentence: _____

   _____

   Equation: _____

5. Laura has 8 cans of hairspray, but wants half that number of cans of hairspray. Write an open sentence for the cans of hairspray c, and then write an equation.

   Open sentence: _____

   _____

   Equation: _____

Check What You Learned

Preparing for Algebra

Read the problem carefully and solve. Show your work under each question.

The local discount store has records of all the items brought in to the store. It also has records of all the items sold. By checking the records, the department managers know how many things to order from suppliers.

1. The clothing manager sees that the weekly sales of some outfits are following a pattern. The pattern is 210, 180, and 150 outfits sold. What are the next three numbers in this pattern?

   _____, _____, _____

2. The recreation department manager sees that 3 times as many tents were sold this week as last week. A total of 18 tents were sold this week. Write an equation to find how many tents were sold last week.

   Equation: _____

3. The housewares department gets a shipment of 70 sets of pans. There are now 125 sets in stock. The supervisor writes an equation to find the number of sets in stock before the shipment. Write the situation as an open sentence. Then, write it as an equation.

   Open sentence: _____

   _____

   Equation: _____

4. The linens supervisor finds that the store sold 1 case of towels plus 12 loose towels one week. She wants to know how many towels were sold in all. What does the variable represent in the situation? Rewrite the situation as a variable expression.

   Variable: _____

   _____

   Variable expression: _____

5. The footwear department sells a truckload of athletic shoes plus 155 pairs during a special sale. The supervisor wants to know the total number of athletic shoes sold during the sale. What does the variable represent in this situation? Write the situation as a variable expression.

   Variable: _____

   _____

   Variable expression: _____

Final Test Chapters 1–13

Read the problem carefully and solve. Show your work under each question.

The Exact Accounting Firm keeps business records for many companies. The companies use the data in the records to keep track of income and expenses. The companies also use the data to plan for the future.

1. Sturdy Roofing Company makes a profit of $120,360 in 6 months. How much profit does the company make each month?

_____ per month

2. Last month, Famous Burger Stop had sales that totaled $43,275. This month, the business had sales that totaled $46,320. What is the difference between the total sales for the two months?

_____

3. Smooth Cut Lawn Service has 81 customers. Each customer pays $924 per year for lawn care. How much money does the lawn service earn each year?

_____ per year

4. Last year, Big Time Corporation employed 5,274 workers. This year, the company adds 378 more workers. How many workers does the company employ now?

_____ workers

5. For the first half of the year, Comfortable Shoes made $67,928 in sales. The second half of the year, the store made $116,457 in sales. How much money did the store make in sales all year?

_____

6. Shiny Kitchenware sold $10,156 worth of products last month. The manager sets a sales goal for the next 18 months based on last month's sales. What is a good estimate of the total sales for the next 18 months?

about _____

Final Test Chapters 1–13

Read the problem carefully and solve. Show your work under each question.

Inventive cooks change recipes to cook food in new ways. Cooks also change recipes to increase or decrease the amount of food they make.

1. Ms. Franklin has a recipe that takes $3\frac{1}{3}$ cups of flour. She wants to reduce the recipe by $\frac{1}{2}$. How much flour is needed for the smaller recipe?

    _____ cups

2. Preston has a recipe that calls for $\frac{3}{5}$ tablespoon of salt. He spills $\frac{1}{6}$ tablespoon by accident. How much salt is left?

    _____ tablespoon

3. Carolyn adds $3\frac{3}{8}$ cups of rice to a mix. She checks the recipe and sees it is $1\frac{1}{4}$ times too much. How much rice should she have added?

    _____ cups

4. Mr. Zhang cooks an egg recipe that needs 0.25 teaspoon of paprika and 0.125 teaspoon of pepper. What is the total amount of these two ingredients?

    _____ teaspoon

5. May mixes punch to serve at a party. The recipe calls for $2\frac{1}{4}$ cups of orange juice. May wants to make $1\frac{2}{3}$ times the recipe. How much orange juice does she need?

    _____ cups

6. Ms. Wilbur thinks about mixing a recipe that has $\frac{1}{7}$ teaspoon of salt with another that has $\frac{1}{5}$ teaspoon of salt. What is the least common multiple of 5 and 7?

    _____

Final Test Chapters 1–13

Read the problem carefully and solve. Show your work under each question.

Impressive Automobile Company makes Mystery Cars. At the factory, the quality workers take measurements while cars are being built. The measurements are done in customary and metric units.

1. The weight of a Mystery Car is 1 ton and 1,453 pounds. How much does the car weigh in pounds?

   _____ lb.

2. The engine of a Mystery Car holds 5 quarts of oil. How much is this volume of oil in pints?

   _____ p.

3. A Mystery Car fits inside a crate that is 2 meters by 2 meters by 5 meters. What is the volume of this crate?

   _____ cu. m

4. A worker records the time it takes to assemble a car. The car assembly starts at 12:03 a.m. It finishes at 9:47 p.m. How long did it take to assemble the car?

   _____ hours _____ minutes

5. A Mystery Car is about 5,000 millimeters long. How long is the car in meters?

   about _____ m

6. The tire of a Mystery Car covers a rectangular area of ground that measures about 18 centimeters by 13 centimeters. What is the area covered?

   about _____ sq. cm

Spectrum Word Problems
Grade 5
108

Final Test
Chapters 1–13

CHAPTERS 1–13 FINAL TEST

Final Test Chapters 1–13

Read the problem carefully and solve. Show your work under each question.

A local sporting goods store sells equipment for camping, hiking, fishing, biking, and golfing. The manager keeps track of the number of sales of most items in the store.

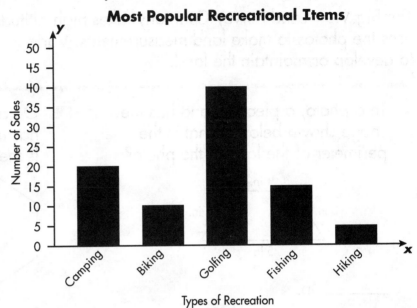

Most Popular Recreational Items

Use the graph to answer questions 1 to 3.

1. How many total items were sold of the two most popular types of recreational equipment?

   _____ items

2. One hour, the cashier has sales of $56, $42, $8, $14, $19, $22, and $42. What is the mean of these sales? What is the mode?

   Mean: _____

   Mode: _____

3. Another time, the cashier has sales of $16, $11, $23, $45, $9, $17, $31, $5, and $15. What is the median of these sales? What is the range?

   Median: _____

   Range: _____

4. Today, there are 6 golfing, 12 fishing, 9 camping, and 3 hiking items on sale. What is the probability that a shopper will buy a fishing item, if the shopper chooses a sale item by chance?

   _____

Spectrum Word Problems
Grade 5

Final Test
Chapters 1–13

109

CHAPTERS 1–13 FINAL TEST

Final Test Chapters 1–13

Read the problem carefully and solve. Show your work under each question.

The Big View Land Survey Company takes high altitude photos of land. The company uses the photos to make land measurements. Various groups use the photos for plans to develop or maintain the land.

1. In a photo, a piece of land has the shape shown below. What is the perimeter of the land in the photo?

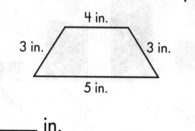

_____ in.

2. A worker marks a photo that looks like the one shown below. What is the figure called?

M   L _____

3. The edges of a field make an angle like the one shown below. What kind of angle is it?

_____

4. On a photo, the roof of a building has the shape shown below. What is the name of this shape?

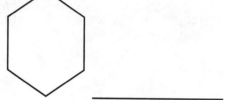

_____

5. From a photo, an analyst finds the dimensions of a building. What is the volume of the building?

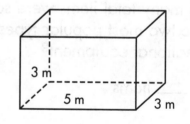

_____ cu. m

6. A typical backyard looks like the figure below. What is this shape called? What is its area?

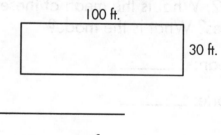

_____

_____ sq. ft.

Final Test Chapters 1–13

Read the problem carefully and solve. Show your work under each question.

The Everything Electronics Store has many electronic device for sale. Shoppers can buy TVs, radios, DVD players, personal music players, and anything else they want. Some employees use ideas from algebra to state business terms.

1. A salesperson says that the store has 3 cases of headphones plus 11 headphones on display. If he writes an expression for the total number of headphones, what would the variable represent in this situation?

_____

_____

2. A salesperson sees a pattern in the last two digits of some ID numbers. The numbers are 46, 57, and 68. What are the next three numbers in this number pattern?

_____, _____, _____

3. A manager writes the following expression for the number of persons p who worked a total of 96 hours in 8-hour shifts. $96 \div p = 8$ Write this equation as an open sentence.

_____

_____

4. The store is selling battery chargers for $22. Write a variable expression for how much money the store will make if it sells x chargers.

_____

5. One employee is scheduled to work 5 days next week and 35 hours in total. The person works the same number of hours each day. Write an equation to express how many hours the person works each day d.

_____

6. The total cost of an electronic photo display comes to $100. The price y plus the tax of $6 equals $100. Write an equation to find the price of the electronic photo display.

_____

Spectrum Word Problems
Grade 5

Final Test
Chapters 1–13

CHAPTERS 1–13 FINAL TEST

111

Scoring Record for Posttests, Mid-Test, and Final Test

Chapter Posttest	Your Score	Performance			
		Excellent	Very Good	Fair	Needs Improvement
1	____ of 6	6	5	3–4	2 or fewer
2	____ of 6	6	5	3–4	2 or fewer
3	____ of 5	5	4	3	2 or fewer
4	____ of 6	6	5	3–4	2 or fewer
5	____ of 6	6	5	3–4	2 or fewer
6	____ of 6	6	5	3–4	2 or fewer
7	____ of 6	6	5	3–4	2 or fewer
8	____ of 6	6	5	3–4	2 or fewer
9	____ of 11	10–11	8–9	6–7	5 or fewer
10	____ of 11	10–11	8–9	6–7	5 or fewer
11	____ of 12	11–12	9–10	7–8	6 or fewer
12	____ of 10	9–10	7–8	5–6	4 or fewer
13	____ of 5	5	4	3	2 or fewer
Mid-Test	____ of 24	22–24	20–21	16–19	15 or fewer
Final Test	____ of 34	33–34	29–32	23–28	22 or fewer

Record your test score in the Your Score column. See where your score falls in the Performance columns. Your score is based on the total number of required responses. If your score is fair or needs improvement, review the chapter material.

Grade 5 Answers

Chapter 1

Pretest, page 1
1. 347
2. 62,023
3. 13,000
4. 315,935
5. 4,598
6. 86,248

Lesson 1.1, page 2
1. 245
2. 59
3. 262
4. 42
5. 209

Lesson 1.2, page 3
1. 267
2. 5,130
3. 575,631
4. 580,494
5. 1,571

Lesson 1.3, page 4
1. 172,155
2. 716,429
3. 397,033
4. 721,908
5. 780,643

Lesson 1.4, page 5
1. 37,000
2. 50,000
3. 2,000
4. 8,000

Posttest, page 6
1. 134,884
2. 91,755
3. 5,399
4. 122,977
5. 220,000
6. 139,295

Chapter 2

Pretest, page 7
1. 9,184
2. 875
3. 17,784
4. 495
5. 54,096
6. 90,000

Lesson 2.1, page 8
1. 113; 339
2. 292
3. 339
4. 54
5. 175

Lesson 2.2, page 9
1. 276
2. 144
3. 1,800
4. 156

Lesson 2.3, page 10
1. $24,750
2. $19,100
3. $24,325
4. $33,750
5. $10,425

Lesson 2.4, page 11
1. 219,840
2. 50,244
3. 293,120
4. 200,976
5. 236,328

Lesson 2.5, page 12
1. 6,000
2. 200
3. 3,000
4. 100

Posttest, page 13
1. 45,360
2. 1,260
3. 5,304
4. 3,500
5. 9,000
6. 945

Chapter 3

Pretest, page 14
1. 8
2. 3
3. 9
4. 20 R27
5. $421

Grade 5 Answers

Lesson 3.1, page 15
1. 2
2. 28
3. 1
4. $2,509

Lesson 3.2, page 16
1. 44
2. 4
3. 15
4. 180
5. $220

Lesson 3.3, page 17
1. 4
2. 3 R8
3. 4
4. 10
5. 7

Lesson 3.4, page 18
1. 75
2. 45
3. 24
4. 21
5. 5

Lesson 3.5, page 19
1. 60
2. 720
3. 110
4. 121

Posttest, page 20
1. $52
2. $60
3. $95
4. 118
5. $112; $26

Chapter 4

Pretest, page 21
1. 7
2. 16
3. $14\frac{2}{3}$
4. $\frac{2}{7}$
5. $2\frac{5}{8}$
6. $\frac{89}{12}$

Lesson 4.1, page 22
1. seven-ninths
2. $\frac{3}{4}$
3. $\frac{3}{7}$
4. five-twelfths
5.

Lesson 4.2, page 23
1. 18
2. 15
3. 8
4. 7
5. 9

Lesson 4.3, page 24
1. $\frac{1}{4}$
2. $\frac{1}{3}$
3. $\frac{1}{2}$
4. $\frac{3}{4}$
5. $\frac{2}{3}$

Lesson 4.4, page 25
1. $8\frac{1}{4}$
2. $10\frac{2}{3}$
3. $5\frac{5}{6}$
4. $6\frac{2}{5}$
5. $7\frac{1}{2}$

Lesson 4.5, page 26
1. $\frac{53}{8}$
2. $\frac{31}{4}$
3. $9\frac{1}{2}$
4. $\frac{33}{4}$
5. $\frac{85}{16}$

Posttest, page 27
1. $\frac{3}{4}$
2. 25
3. $4\frac{2}{3}$
4. 11
5. $2\frac{4}{7}$
6. $4\frac{1}{3}$

Grade 5 Answers

Chapter 5

Pretest, page 28

1. $\frac{1}{2}$
2. $\frac{9}{20}$
3. $1\frac{1}{2}$
4. $\frac{21}{40}$
5. $\frac{7}{16}$
6. $\frac{13}{24}$

Lesson 5.1, page 29

1. $1\frac{1}{2}$
2. $\frac{2}{3}$
3. $\frac{1}{2}$
4. $1\frac{1}{3}$
5. $\frac{3}{4}$

Lesson 5.2, page 30

1. $\frac{8}{10}$
2. $\frac{24}{8}$
3. $\frac{10}{15}$
4. $\frac{3}{21}$
5. $\frac{30}{15}$

Lesson 5.3, page 31

1. $\frac{11}{15}$
2. $\frac{37}{56}$
3. $\frac{19}{20}$
4. $\frac{55}{63}$
5. $1\frac{5}{8}$

Lesson 5.4, page 32

1. $4\frac{1}{4}$
2. $9\frac{7}{12}$
3. Catherine
4. $9\frac{7}{20}$
5. $6\frac{5}{6}$

Posttest, page 33

1. $\frac{7}{16}$
2. $1\frac{31}{40}$
3. $\frac{2}{3}$
4. 1
5. $\frac{3}{12}$
6. $1\frac{61}{88}$

Chapter 6

Pretest, page 34

1. $\frac{7}{9}$
2. $\frac{3}{4}$
3. $2\frac{3}{5}$
4. 0.625
5. $2\frac{2}{3}$
6. 1.8

Lesson 6.1, page 35

1. $\frac{3}{5}$
2. $\frac{2}{3}$
3. $\frac{1}{4}$
4. $\frac{5}{7}$
5. $\frac{5}{9}$

Lesson 6.2, page 36

1. $6\frac{1}{3}$
2. $4\frac{4}{9}$
3. $2\frac{8}{15}$
4. $3\frac{7}{12}$
5. $7\frac{1}{3}$

Lesson 6.3, page 37

1. $3\frac{1}{2}$
2. $4\frac{1}{7}$
3. $5\frac{2}{3}$
4. $1\frac{1}{3}$
5. $3\frac{7}{11}$

Grade 5 Answers

Lesson 6.4, page 38

1. $\frac{7}{15}$
2. $\frac{17}{24}$
3. $\frac{13}{30}$
4. $\frac{16}{35}$
5. $\frac{47}{72}$

Lesson 6.5, page 39

1. $4\frac{1}{2}$
2. $1\frac{1}{2}$
3. $\frac{53}{63}$
4. $1\frac{5}{6}$
5. $7\frac{54}{77}$

Lesson 6.6, page 40

1. 7
2. 3
3. $8.14 < 8.41$
4. 9

Lesson 6.7, page 41

1. 5.14
2. $15.40
3. 4
4. $23
5. 4.2

Lesson 6.8, page 42

1. 0.89
2. 93.85
3. 7.49
4. 3.5
5. 2.61

Lesson 6.9, page 43

1. $5.30
2. 10 for $17.42
3. $78.84
4. 176.16
5. 140.58
6. 1.20

Posttest, page 44

1. $\frac{1}{3}$
2. 0.375
3. $7\frac{2}{7}$
4. $\frac{1}{30}$
5. $\frac{23}{30}$
6. $\frac{1}{14}$

Mid-Test

page 45

1. 165
2. 39,268
3. 45,047
4. 59,000
5. 118,816
6. 732,870

page 46

1. 193; 3
2. 1,458
3. 15,255
4. 17; 12
5. 48,944
6. 1,050

page 47

1. $\frac{3}{4}$
2. $\frac{31}{7}$
3. $3\frac{2}{15}$
4. 2
5. 9
6. $\frac{29}{8}$

page 48

1. 13.8
2. $1\frac{1}{2}$
3. $5\frac{5}{6}$
4. 3.3
5. $2\frac{1}{2}$
6. $1\frac{5}{12}$

Grade 5 Answers

Chapter 7

Pretest, page 49

1. $\frac{7}{8}$
2. 5
3. $1\frac{11}{12}$
4. $\frac{3}{40}$
5. 17
6. 23

Lesson 7.1, page 50

1. $12\frac{3}{4}$
2. 34
3. $14\frac{2}{3}$
4. 26
5. 69

Lesson 7.2, page 51

1. $14\frac{2}{5}$
2. $9\frac{5}{8}$
3. $5\frac{2}{15}$
4. $15\frac{5}{9}$
5. $2\frac{5}{8}$

Lesson 7.3, page 52

1. $\frac{7}{10}$
2. $1058\frac{4}{7}$ square yards
3. $\frac{5}{22}$
4. $\frac{7}{40}$
5. $594\frac{65}{72}$ square yards

Posttest, page 53

1. $3\frac{7}{8}$
2. 14
3. $25\frac{1}{2}$
4. $3\frac{3}{5}$
5. $2\frac{5}{8}$
6. $5\frac{5}{8}$

Chapter 8

Pretest, page 54

1. 40
2. $\frac{1}{6}$
3. $4\frac{16}{21}$
4. 28
5. 32
6. $13\frac{1}{5}$

Lesson 8.1, page 55

1. $2\frac{5}{14}$
2. $\frac{4}{3}$
3. $2\frac{2}{9}$
4. $1\frac{9}{10}$
5. 32

Lesson 8.2, page 56

1. $\frac{3}{4}$
2. $3\frac{3}{5}$
3. $\frac{2}{3}$
4. $9\frac{1}{3}$
5. $7\frac{6}{7}$

Lesson 8.3, page 57

1. $1\frac{3}{5}$
2. $\frac{15}{31}$
3. $\frac{10}{27}$
4. $\frac{3}{7}$
5. $\frac{25}{31}$

Lesson 8.4, page 58

1. 7; 2; 3; draw 7 ×s over $\frac{1}{4}$, 2 ×s over $\frac{1}{2}$, and 3 ×s over $\frac{3}{4}$
2. $1\frac{3}{4}$
3. 1
4. $2\frac{1}{4}$
5. 5
6. $\frac{5}{12}$

Grade 5 Answers

Posttest, page 59

1. $3\frac{1}{11}$
2. 48
3. $\frac{1}{16}$
4. 56
5. $2\frac{5}{8}$
6. 52

Chapter 9

Pretest, page 60

1. 43
2. 12
3. 6
4. 72
5. 3
6. 122

Pretest, page 61

1. 42
2. 38
3. 63
4. 1; 44
5. 48

Lesson 9.1, page 62

1. 259
2. 80
3. 5,316
4. 5
5. 2,524

Lesson 9.2, page 63

1. 56
2. 15
3. 6
4. 5
5. 25

Lesson 9.3, page 64

1. 38
2. 5
3. 4,650
4. 12
5. 15

Lesson 9.4, page 65

1.

2. 79
3.

4. 68

Lesson 9.5, page 66

1. 5; 15
2. 4; 46
3. 2; 35
4. 1; 41

Lesson 9.6, page 67

1. 25
2. 36
3. 12
4. 40

Lesson 9.7, page 68

1. 216
2. 12
3. 27
4. 36
5. 90

Lesson 9.8, page 69

1. answers will vary
2. 147
3. 186
4. 138

Posttest, page 70

1. 7
2. 114
3. 5,530
4. 165
5. 5
6. 4

Grade 5 Answers

Posttest, page 71

1. 6; 24
2. 864
3. 126
4. 35°
5. 16; 15

Chapter 10

Pretest, page 72

1. 16,000
2. 3
3. 9,000
4. 15
5. 123
6. 1,140

Pretest, page 73

1. 35
2. 36; 81
3. 4,320
4. 28
5. 144

Lesson 10.1, page 74

1. 5,000
2. 220
3. 650
4. 900,000
5. 20,000

Lesson 10.2, page 75

1. 12,000
2. 4
3. 3,000
4. 60 L
5. 50

Lesson 10.3, page 76

1. 50,000,000
2. 70
3. 2,000
4. 4
5. 3,000

Lesson 10.4, page 77

1. 11
2.

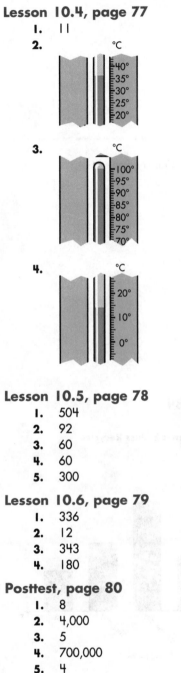

Lesson 10.5, page 78

1. 504
2. 92
3. 60
4. 60
5. 300

Lesson 10.6, page 79

1. 336
2. 12
3. 343
4. 180

Posttest, page 80

1. 8
2. 4,000
3. 5
4. 700,000
5. 4
6. 270,000

Grade 5 Answers

Posttest, page 81
1. 5
2. 316
3. 5,341
4. 42
5. 150,000

Chapter 11

Pretest, page 82
1. Rock, Rap, R&B, Country, Pop
2. 25
3. 5
4. 55
5. 15
6. 105

Pretest, page 83
1. 25
2. 20
3. 27
4. 26
5. $\frac{1}{7}$
6. $\frac{2}{7}$

Lesson 11.1, page 84
1.

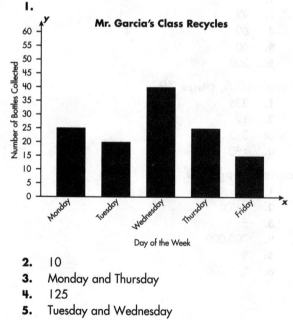

2. 10
3. Monday and Thursday
4. 125
5. Tuesday and Wednesday

Lesson 11.2, page 85
1.

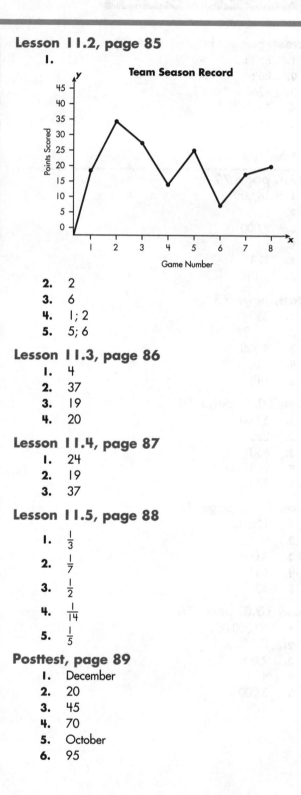

2. 2
3. 6
4. 1; 2
5. 5; 6

Lesson 11.3, page 86
1. 4
2. 37
3. 19
4. 20

Lesson 11.4, page 87
1. 24
2. 19
3. 37

Lesson 11.5, page 88
1. $\frac{1}{3}$
2. $\frac{1}{7}$
3. $\frac{1}{2}$
4. $\frac{1}{14}$
5. $\frac{1}{5}$

Posttest, page 89
1. December
2. 20
3. 45
4. 70
5. October
6. 95

Grade 5 Answers

Posttest, page 90

1. 27
2. 40
3. 31
4. 42
5. $\frac{2}{7}$
6. $\frac{1}{7}$

Chapter 12

Pretest, page 91

1. line, $\overleftrightarrow{ST}$
2. parallel
3. $\overrightarrow{KL}$
4. (5, 6)
5. (2, 4)
6. label point C at (9, 9)

Pretest, page 92

1. parallelogram
2. square
3. curved, flat
4. trapezoid
5. hexagon
6. rectangle

Lesson 12.1, page 93

1. 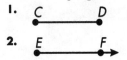 C   D

2. E   F

3. K   L

4. $\overrightarrow{ED}$; $\overrightarrow{EF}$; E; ∠DEF
5. ∠456; $\overrightarrow{54}$; $\overrightarrow{56}$; 5

Lesson 12.2, page 94

1. (4, 5)
2. (6, 7)
3. plot point C at (2, 10)
4. plot point E at (9, 4)
2. (4, 2)
2. plot point B at (9, 11)

Lesson 12.3, page 95

1. parallel
2. intersecting
3.

4. perpendicular
5.

Lesson 12.4, page 96

1. cylinder
2. circles
3. cube
4. 12; 6; 8

Posttest, page 97

1. perpendicular lines
2. ∠GHI; obtuse
3. line segment; $\overline{CD}$
4. 87°
5. parallel lines
6. ∠RST; acute

Posttest, page 98

1. kite
2. rectangular pyramid; 5
3. parallelogram
4. rectangular prism; 6; 12

Chapter 13

Pretest, page 99

1. 66; 77
2. the number of headlights in a box
3. t minus 12 equals 25
4. the number of cans on a shelf; x + 8
5. 367; 370; 373

Lesson 13.1, page 100

1. 7843
2. 29; 36; 44; 53
3. 66; 60; 54
4. $22; $15; $8
5. 26; 42; 68

Grade 5 Answers

Lesson 13.2, page 101
1. 13
2. 3
3. 35
4. 17

Lesson 13.3, page 102
1. (0, 0), (1, 4), (2, 8), (3, 12), (4, 16), and (5, 20)
2.
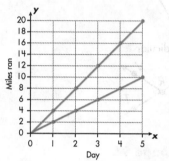
3. Marcia
4. Since Marcia runs 4 miles more each day than the day before, and Greg runs 2 miles more than the day before, Marcia's number of miles is always greater.

Lesson 13.4, page 103
1. number of potatoes in a bag; $x + 5$
2. number of muffins in a tray; $x + 6$
3. number of cans of soup in a case; $x - 2$
4. number of bananas in a bunch; $b + 8$

Lesson 13.5, page 104
1. x plus 11 equals 24; $x + 11 = 24$
2. p plus 9 equals 12; $p + 9 = 12$
3. t minus 3 equals 6; $t - 3 = 6$
4. 4 times x equals 24; $4x = 24$
5. 8 divided by 2 equals c; $\frac{8}{2} = c$

Posttest, page 105
1. 120; 90; 60
2. $3x = 18$; $x = 6$
3. x plus 70 equals 125; $x + 70 = 125$
4. the number of towels in a case; $x + 12$
5. the number of shoes in a truckload; $x + 155$

Final Test

page 106
1. $20,060
2. $3,045
3. $74,844
4. 5,652
5. $184,385
6. $180,000 or $200,000

page 107
1. $1\frac{2}{3}$
2. $\frac{13}{30}$
3. $2\frac{7}{10}$
4. 0.375
5. $3\frac{3}{4}$
6. 35

page 108
1. 3,453
2. 10
3. 20
4. 21; 44
5. 5
6. 234

page 109
1. 60
2. $29; $42
3. $16; $40
4. $\frac{2}{5}$

page 110
1. 15
2. line
3. acute angle
4. hexagon
5. 45
6. rectangle; 3,000

page 111
1. the number of headphones in a case
2. 79; 90; 101
3. 96 divided by p equals 8
4. $22x
5. 5d 5 35
6. y | $6 5 $100

Notes